How To Handle

A Small Lot

A quick peek at our cover home will show you that even the smallest homes can pack big style

See more about our cover home, Plan #598-052D-0121, on page 33. This home exemplifies efficient design, making every use of space to ensure this home is packed with the elegance and convenience that every small home needs. Make this home yours by following our easy ordering information on page 256.

Contradictory to the rampant idea of "bigger is better" more people are investing in small lots to build their dream homes. For some it is most affordable, others desire proximity to specific locales, and some see small lots as a way to reduce their ecological footprint.

Whatever the reason, the same is true for all – smaller lots are not about less space. It is intelligent building with some extra creativity thrown in for good measure. The challenges presented by building on small lots are nothing to be discouraged by, and the sacrifices are less than one may anticipate. Think new options rather than fewer options!

Small lots are considered to be 50 feet (or less) wide. The home plans included in this collection are 40 feet (or less) wide and extend as far as 85 feet in depth, with the extra lot space accounting for the driveway and garage placement on the side or rear. Small lot homes can be positioned in a variety of

ways to maximize the land use. The most efficient use of space for a small lot home is building two stories. This is more economical as there will be greater space without additional foundation or roofing expenses.

Small lot homes often have small yards that homeowners choose to landscape creatively, accent with cozy porches, or convert to larger patios that allow for perfect entertaining possibilities. If small home lots are grouped together, a community courtyard may be in place rather than individual yards, with garages accessed from the rear via an alleyway. Along with yards, garages are typically the greatest challenge to small lot designers. In addition to highly functional rear garages, front garages with accented doors eliminate excessive driveway space without diminishing the home's beauty.

Inside small lot homes, efficiency is at a premium. Every nook and cranny is used to its fullest potential, eliminating storage concerns and dread of lost personal space. Even windows are placed strategically, some allowing five times more light inside, expanding the home's spatial feel. Design is just as significant, if not more so, in comparison to size.

Small lot homes are not inferior, limiting, or restricted to uniformity. They are quite capable of being fully accessorized inside and out, in addition to being particularly affordable. Dream homes, like dreams themselves, come in all sizes.

Photo right: This enchanting master bath pampers the homeowners, and multiple windows bring in an abundance of light, making the space appear even larger.

Photo below: A fireplace, built-in shelves and French doors to a screened porch decorate this living room. With the right touches, smaller homes can offer all the same amenities found in a larger home.

Home Plans *for a* smaller lot

over **240** home plans

Plan #598-055D-0046
is featured on page 32.
Photo courtesy of
Nelson Design Group.

Plan #598-016D-0029
is featured on page 8.
Photo courtesy of
Perfect Home Plans.

Plan #598-052D-0051
is featured on page 18.
Photo courtesy of Jannis
Vann & Associates, Inc.

Plan #598-026D-0161
is featured on page 30.
Photo courtesy of
Design Basics, Inc.

Home Plans for a Smaller Lot is published by HDA, Inc., 944 Anglum Road, St. Louis, MO 63042.
All rights reserved. Reproduction in whole or part without written permission of the
publisher is prohibited. Printed in the U.S.A. © 2007.

COVER HOME - The main home shown on the front cover is Plan #598-052D-0121 and is
featured on page 33. Photo courtesy of Jannis Vann & Associates, Inc.

Current Printing   5   4   3   2

Home Plans *for a* smaller lot

Browse this selection of over 240 home plans for a smaller lot and discover endless possibilities of exterior and interior design elements that make each home feel custom. This assortment of charming homes includes styles with character and function all in one

Special features

- 1,268 total square feet of living area
- Multiple gables, large porch and arched windows create a classy exterior
- Innovative design provides openness in the great room, kitchen and breakfast room
- Secondary bedrooms have private hall with bath
- 3 bedrooms, 2 baths, 2-car garage
- Basement foundation, drawings also include crawl space and slab foundations

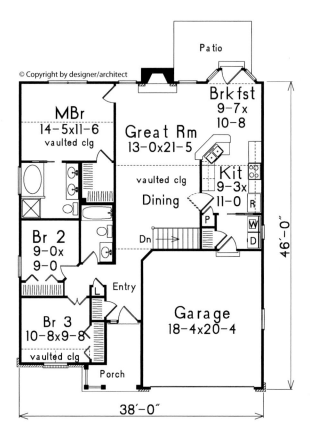

© Copyright by designer/architect

MBr
14-5x11-6
vaulted clg

Brkfst
9-7x
10-8

Great Rm
13-0x21-5

vaulted clg

Kit
9-3x
11-0

Dining

Br 2
9-0x
9-0

Dn

46'-0"

Entry

Br 3
10-8x9-8
vaulted clg

Garage
18-4x20-4

Patio

Porch

38'-0"

Rear Elevation

Special features

- 1,635 total square feet of living area
- Large wrap-around front porch
- Open living and dining rooms are separated only by columns for added openness
- Kitchen includes a large work island and snack bar
- Master bedroom with tray ceiling has three closets
- 3 bedrooms, 2 1/2 baths, 2-car garage
- Basement, crawl space or slab foundation, please specify when ordering

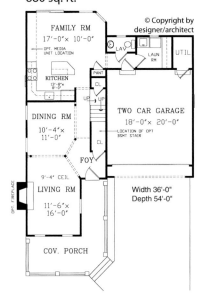

First Floor
880 sq. ft.

© Copyright by designer/architect

FAMILY RM
17'-0" × 10'-0"

OPT. MEDIA
UNIT LOCATION

LAV.

LAUN
RM

UTIL

KITCHEN
13'-8"×
8'-0"

PANT

CL

UP UP

DINING RM
10'-4"×
11'-0"

TWO CAR GARAGE
18'-0"× 20'-0"

LOCATION OF OPT
BSMT STAIR

CL

FOY

9'-4" CEIL

OPT. FIREPLACE

LIVING RM
11'-6"×
16'-0"

Width 36'-0"
Depth 54'-0"

COV. PORCH

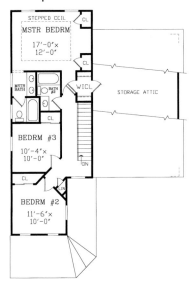

Second Floor
755 sq. ft.

STEPPED CEIL

CL

MSTR BEDRM
17'-0"×
12'-0"

CL

MSTR
BATH

BATH
#2

WICL

STORAGE ATTIC

CL

BEDRM #3
10'-4"×
10'-0"

DN

CL

BEDRM #2
11'-6"×
10'-0"

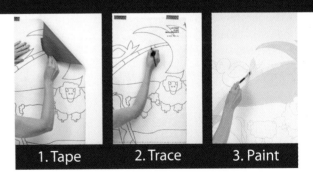

Special features

- 1,710 total square feet of living area
- Energy efficient home with 2" x 6" exterior walls
- Clerestory windows brighten second floor and living room below
- Lower level recreation room includes a luxurious whirlpool tub and wet bar
- Unique centered fireplace separates dining and living rooms
- 3 bedrooms, 2 baths, 1-car drive under garage
- Basement foundation

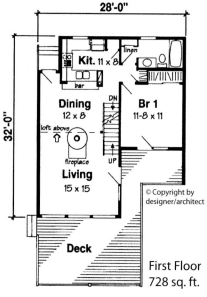

28'-0"

32'-0"

Kit. 11 x 8
linen
bar
Dining 12 x 8
DN
Br 1 11-8 x 11
loft above
fireplace
UP
Living 15 x 15

© Copyright by designer/architect

Deck

First Floor
728 sq. ft.

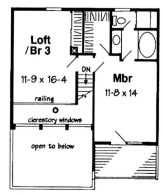

Loft /Br 3 11-9 x 16-4
DN
Mbr 11-8 x 14
railing
clerestory windows
open to below

Second Floor
573 sq. ft.

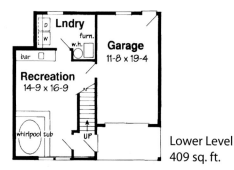

Lndry
furn.
D
W
w.h.
Garage 11-8 x 19-4
bar
Recreation 14-9 x 16-9
whirlpool tub
UP

Lower Level
409 sq. ft.

Alternate Rear View

Many of our customers ask the question, "Do you know a Builder in my area?"

We now have the ability to put our customers in touch with builders that purchase plans from HDA.

This exclusive service is offered to members of the FREE **Builder's Advantage Program**

Members will be eligible for the following Program Benefits:

• Locate a Builder Network

• FREE Shipping

• Discounted Material Lists

• Software Plan Package

• Toll-Free Builder Phone Line

• FREE Home Plan Books

• 10% Plan Discount

This is a FREE service that will benefit both the customer and the builder. That's the…

To join, visit:

www.houseplansandmore.com

Special features

- 1,553 total square feet of living area
- Two-story living area creates an open and airy feel to the interior especially with two dormers above
- First floor master bedroom is private and includes its own bath and walk-in closet
- Two secondary bedrooms share a full bath with double vanity
- 3 bedrooms, 2 1/2 baths, 2-car drive under garage
- Walk-out basement foundation

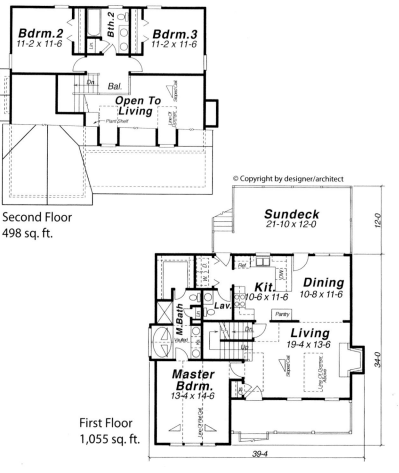

Bdrm.2
11-2 x 11-6

Bth.2

Bdrm.3
11-2 x 11-6

Lin.

Dn.   Bal.

Open To Living

Plant Shelf

Sloped Ceil.

Line Of Dormer

Second Floor
498 sq. ft.

Sundeck
21-10 x 12-0

12-0

Ref.

W. D.

Kit.
10-6 x 11-6

DW

Dining
10-8 x 11-6

Lav.

Pantry

M.Bath

Vaulted

Dn.

Up

Living
19-4 x 13-6

Sloped Ceil.

Line Of Dormer Above

34-0

Master Bdrm.
13-4 x 14-6

Line Of Flat Ceil.

First Floor
1,055 sq. ft.

39-4

Special features

- 1,644 total square feet of living area
- Energy efficient home with 2" x 6" exterior walls
- A highly versatile great room with a wrap-around covered porch encourages relaxed entertaining and is perfectly suited for evolving family activities
- The large U-shaped kitchen with raised breakfast bar is open to the great room ensuring that everyone is included in the fun
- The second floor vaulted studio has a private covered balcony and easily transforms this space into a home office
- 2 bedrooms, 2 baths
- Crawl space foundation

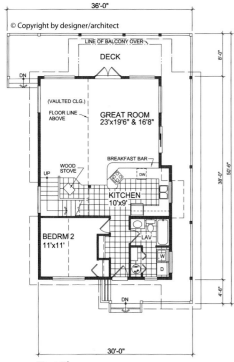

First Floor
955 sq. ft.

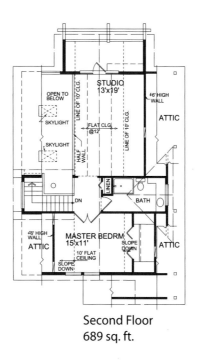

Second Floor
689 sq. ft.

Special features

- 1,848 total square feet of living area
- Kitchen is conveniently located near the dining area
- Great room has a fireplace and built-in bookshelves
- Kid's nook near laundry room includes bench with storage and hanging clothes space
- Master suite has a sitting area
- 3 bedrooms, 2 baths, 2-car rear entry garage
- Crawl space or slab foundation, please specify when ordering

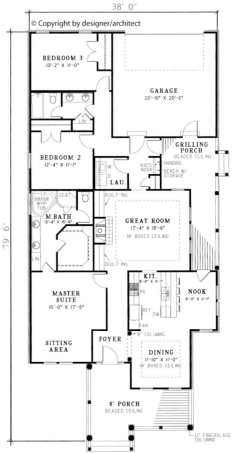

38' 0"

© Copyright by designer/architect

BEDROOM 3
13'-2" X 11'-0"

GARAGE
20'-10" X 20'-0"

LIN.

GRILLING
PORCH
BEADED CEILING

BEDROOM 2
12'-4" X 11'-1"

W
D
LAU.

KID'S
NOOK

HANGING

BENCH W/
STORAGE

60X60
WHP
TUB

SEAT

BUILT-INS

GREAT ROOM
17'-4" X 15'-6"
10' BOXED CEILING

M.BATH
12'-4" X 15'-6"

LIN.

BUILT-INS

KIT.
9'-8" X 11'-1"

NOOK
8'-0" X 11'-1"

RG

REF DW

PAN

MASTER
SUITE
15'-0" X 17'-5"

FOYER

SITTING
AREA

8' COLUMNS

DINING
11'-10" X 11'-0"
10' BOXED CEILING

79' 6"

8' PORCH
BEADED CEILING

12" FIBERGLASS
COLUMNS

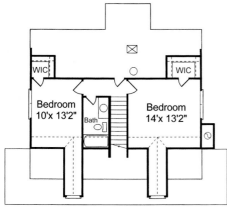

Second Floor
572 sq. ft.

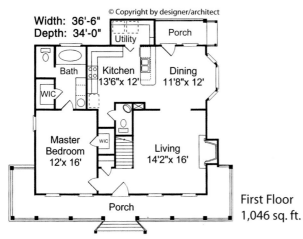

First Floor
1,046 sq. ft.

Special features

- 1,618 total square feet of living area
- Secondary bedrooms with walk-in closets are located on the second floor and share a bath
- Utility room is tucked away in the kitchen for convenience but is out of sight
- Dining area is brightened by a large bay window
- 3 bedrooms, 2 1/2 baths
- Slab or crawl space foundation, please specify when ordering

Special features

- 2,076 total square feet of living area
- The cozy breakfast room enjoys a built-in desk and sliding glass doors extending the dining possibilities to the outdoors
- The second floor enjoys two balcony views of the spacious first floor
- All bedrooms include walk-in closets for easy organization
- 3 bedrooms, 2 1/2 baths, 2-car garage
- Basement foundation

First Floor
1,117 sq. ft.

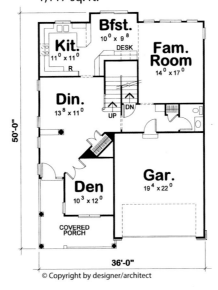

Bfst.
10^0 x 9^8
DESK

Kit.
11^0 x 11^0

R

Fam.
Room
14^0 x 17^0

Din.
13^8 x 11^0

UP   DN

Den
10^3 x 12^0

Gar.
19^4 x 22^0

COVERED
PORCH

50'-0"

36'-0"

Second Floor
959 sq. ft.

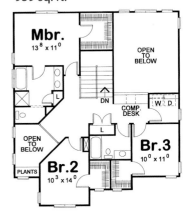

Mbr.
13^8 x 11^0

OPEN
TO
BELOW

L

DN

COMP.
DESK

W D

OPEN
TO
BELOW

L

PLANTS

Br.2
10^3 x 14^0

Br.3
10^0 x 11^0

Special features

- 1,189 total square feet of living area
- All bedrooms are located on the second floor
- Dining room and kitchen both have views of the patio
- Convenient half bath is located near the kitchen
- Master bedroom has a private bath
- 3 bedrooms, 2 1/2 baths, 2-car garage
- Basement foundation

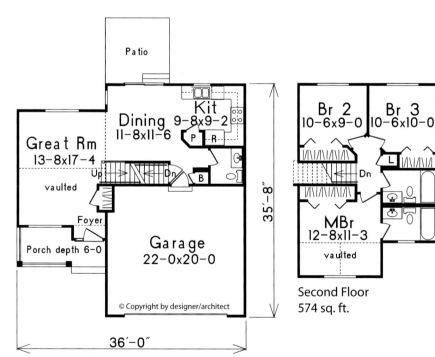

Patio

Kit
9-8x9-2

Dining
11-8x11-6

P   R

Great Rm
13-8x17-4

Up   Dn

B

vaulted

Foyer

Porch depth 6-0

Garage
22-0x20-0

© Copyright by designer/architect

36'-0"

First Floor
615 sq. ft.

Br 2
10-6x9-0

Br 3
10-6x10-0

L

Dn

MBr
12-8x11-3

vaulted

35'-8"

Second Floor
574 sq. ft.

Rear Elevation

Special features

- 1,929 total square feet of living area
- Luxurious master bath has an enormous spa tub with surrounding shelves and double vanities
- Spacious laundry room has counterspace for folding
- Breakfast area has a handy desk
- 3 bedrooms, 2 1/2 baths, 2-car garage
- Walk-out basement foundation

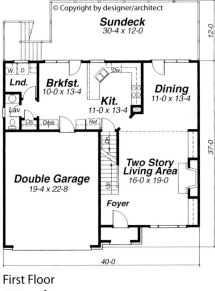

© Copyright by designer/architect

Sundeck 30-4 x 12-0

12-0

W. D.

Lnd.

Brkfst. 10-0 13-4

Dw.

Kit. 11-0 x 13-4

Dining 11-0 x 13-4

Lav.

Cts. Desk Ref.

37-0

Double Garage 19-4 x 22-8

Two Story Living Area 16-0 x 19-0

Foyer

40-0

First Floor
946 sq. ft.

Bdrm.3 12-0 x 11-4

Bath 2

Bdrm.2 11-0 x 13-4

Lin.

Master Bdrm. 13-4 x 16-4

Open To Living Area

M.Bath

Second Floor
983 sq. ft.

Special features

- 1,516 total square feet of living area
- All living and dining areas are interconnected for a spacious look and easy movement
- Covered entrance leads into the sunken great room with a rugged corner fireplace
- Second floor loft opens to rooms below and can convert to a third bedroom
- The dormer in bedroom #2 adds interest
- 2 bedrooms, 2 1/2 baths, 2-car garage
- Basement foundation

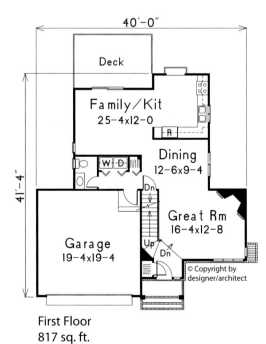

40'-0"

41'-4"

Deck

Family/Kit
25-4x12-0

Dining
12-6x9-4

W D

Dn

Up

Dn

Great Rm
16-4x12-8

Garage
19-4x19-4

© Copyright by designer/architect

First Floor
817 sq. ft.

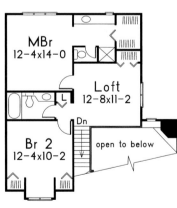

MBr
12-4x14-0

Loft
12-8x11-2

L

Dn

Br 2
12-4x10-2

open to below

Second Floor
699 sq. ft.

Rear Elevation

Special features

- 2,051 total square feet of living area
- A corner fireplace warms the kitchen, family and breakfast rooms
- The private master bedroom enjoys a deluxe bath with double-bowl vanity and whirlpool tub and a nearby walk-in closet
- The spacious secondary bedrooms share a full bath and computer loft
- The unfinished storage area on the second floor has an additional 376 square feet of living area
- 3 bedrooms, 2 1/2 baths, 2-car garage
- Basement foundation

First Floor
1,497 sq. ft.

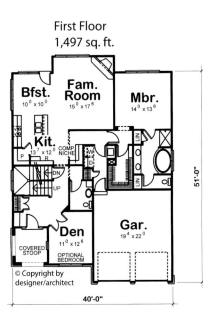

Second Floor
554 sq. ft.

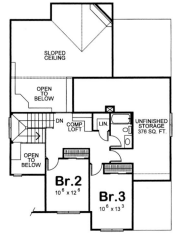

Special features

- 1,328 total square feet of living area
- Wall of windows brightens the living room
- An open living area is created on the first floor with the kitchen and dining area combining with the living room
- Master bedroom is located on the second floor for privacy
- 3 bedrooms, 2 baths
- Basement, crawl space or slab foundation, please specify when ordering

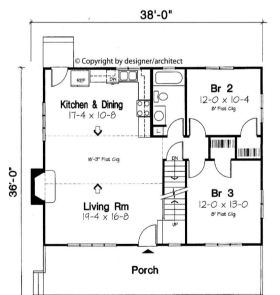

38'-0"

© Copyright by designer/architect

REF   DW

Kitchen & Dining
17-4 x 10-8

16'-3" Flat Clg

DN

Living Rm
19-4 x 16-8

UP

Porch

36'-0"

Br 2
12-0 x 10-4
8' Flat Clg

Br 3
12-0 x 13-0
8' Flat Clg

First Floor
1,013 sq. ft.

Open to Living Room Below

DN

Flat Clg @ 7'-6"

Master Br
12-0 x 13-4

Second Floor
315 sq. ft.

Rear View

Special features

- 1,768 total square feet of living area
- Upon entering you will get a feeling of spaciousness with the two-story living and dining rooms
- The bayed breakfast area is a refreshing place to start the day
- The covered porch off the breakfast area extends the dining to the outdoors
- 3 bedrooms, 2 1/2 baths
- Slab or crawl space foundation, please specify when ordering

First Floor
1,247 sq. ft.

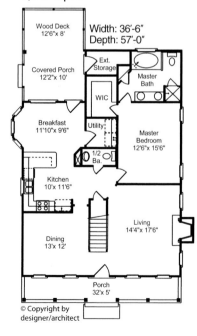

Width: 36'-6"
Depth: 57'-0"

Wood Deck 12'6"x 8'

Covered Porch 12'2"x 10'

Ext. Storage

Master Bath

WIC

Breakfast 11'10"x 9'6"

Utility

Master Bedroom 12'6"x 15'6"

1/2 Ba.

Kitchen 10'x 11'6"

Dining 13'x 12'

Living 14'4"x 17'6"

Porch 32'x 5'

© Copyright by designer/architect

Second Floor
521 sq. ft.

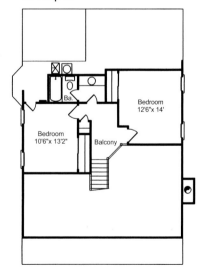

Ba.

Bedroom 12'6"x 14'

Bedroom 10'6"x 13'2"

Balcony

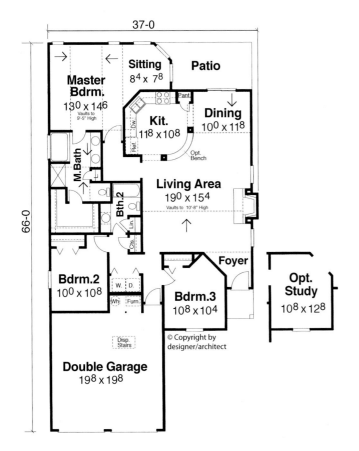

37-0

Sitting
8⁴ x 7⁸

Patio

Master
Bdrm.
13⁰ x 14⁶
Vaults to
9'-5" High

Kit.
11⁸ x 10⁸

Dining
10⁰ x 11⁸

Opt. Bench

M.Bath

Living Area
19⁰ x 15⁴
Vaults to 10'-8" High

Bth.2

66-0

Bdrm.2
10⁰ x 10⁸

W. D.
Whl Furn.

Foyer

Bdrm.3
10⁸ x 10⁴

Opt.
Study
10⁸ x 12⁸

Disp.
Stairs

© Copyright by
designer/architect

Double Garage
19⁸ x 19⁸

Special features

- 1,532 total square feet of living area
- Master bedroom features a private bath with walk-in closet and a sitting area overlooking the outdoor patio
- Bedroom #3 can easily be converted to a study with an additional entrance near the foyer
- The kitchen design includes an option for a curved bench creating more space for dining if needed
- 3 bedrooms, 2 baths, 2-car garage
- Basement or slab foundation, please specify when ordering

Side View

Special features

- 1,568 total square feet of living area
- Covered porch invites guests into the home and opens to the large family room with fireplace and built-ins
- A large island adds workspace to the kitchen and connects to the breakfast area
- The second floor houses the bedrooms and an unfinished storage area that has an additional 327 square feet of living area
- 3 bedrooms, 2 1/2 baths, 2-car garage
- Basement foundation

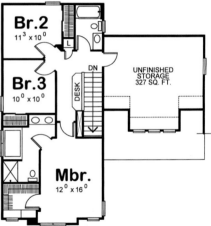

Second Floor
781 sq. ft.

Br.2
$11^3 \times 10^0$

DN

UNFINISHED
STORAGE
327 SQ. FT.

Br.3
$10^0 \times 10^0$

DESK

Mbr.
$12^0 \times 16^0$

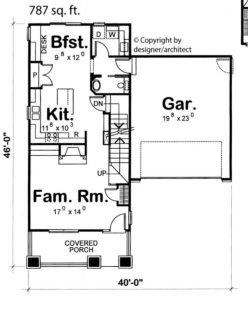

First Floor
787 sq. ft.

DESK

Bfst.
$9^8 \times 12^0$

D   W

© Copyright by
designer/architect

P

Kit.
$11^8 \times 10^3$

DN

Gar.
$19^8 \times 23^0$

R

UP

46'-0"

Fam. Rm.
$17^0 \times 14^0$

COVERED
PORCH

40'-0"

Special features

- 1,470 total square feet of living area
- Vaulted breakfast room is cheerful and sunny
- Private second floor master bedroom has a bath and walk-in closet
- Large utility room has access to the outdoors
- 3 bedrooms, 2 baths
- Basement, crawl space or slab foundation, please specify when ordering

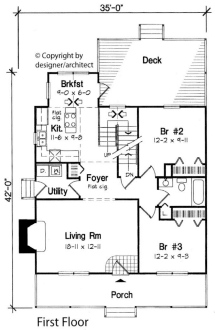

35'-0"

© Copyright by designer/architect

Deck

Brkfst
9-0 x 6-0

Flat clg.

Kit.
11-6 x 9-8

Br #2
12-2 x 9-11

UP

DN

Foyer
Flat clg.

Utility

42'-0"

Living Rm
18-11 x 12-11

Br #3
12-2 x 9-3

Porch

First Floor
1,035 sq. ft.

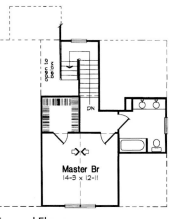

open to below

DN

Master Br
14-3 x 12-11

Second Floor
435 sq. ft.

Rear View

Special features

- 1,577 total square feet of living area
- A well-organized kitchen has a conveniently located laundry room and work desk
- A bright and cheerful living room has lots of windows and a cozy fireplace
- Vaulted master bedroom has a walk-in closet as well as a private bath
- 3 bedrooms, 2 1/2 baths, 2-car garage
- Basement or slab foundation, please specify when ordering

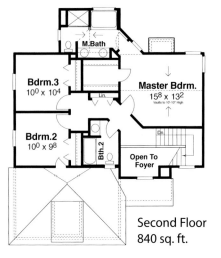

Second Floor
840 sq. ft.

M.Bath

Bdrm.3
10^0 x 10^4

Master Bdrm.
15^8 x 13^2
Vaults to 10'-10" High

Bdrm.2
10^0 x 9^8

Bth.2

Open To Foyer

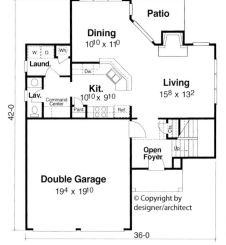

Patio

Dining
10^{10} x 11^0

Laund.

Lav.

Kit.
10^{10} x 9^{10}

Command Center

Pant

Ref.

Living
15^8 x 13^2

Open Foyer

Up

Double Garage
19^4 x 19^{10}

42-0

36-0

© Copyright by designer/architect

First Floor
737 sq. ft.

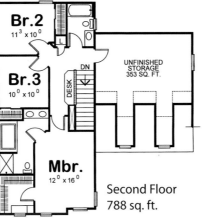

Br.2
11³ x 10⁰

Br.3
10⁰ x 10⁰

L

DN

DESK

UNFINISHED
STORAGE
353 SQ. FT.

Mbr.
12⁰ x 16⁰

Second Floor
788 sq. ft.

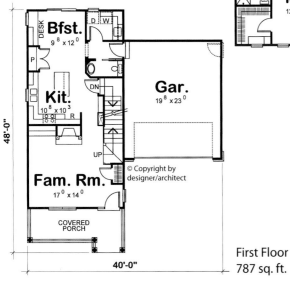

DESK

Bfst.
9⁸ x 12⁰

D   W

P

Kit.
10⁸ x 10³

DN

R

Gar.
19⁸ x 23⁰

UP

Fam. Rm.
17⁰ x 14⁰

© Copyright by
designer/architect

COVERED
PORCH

48'-0"

40'-0"

First Floor
787 sq. ft.

Special features

- 1,575 total square feet of living area
- A half bath is tucked away in the laundry area for convenience
- Second floor hall has a handy desk
- Bonus area on the second floor has an additional 353 square feet of living area
- 3 bedrooms, 2 1/2 baths, 2-car garage
- Basement foundation

Special features

- 1,556 total square feet of living area
- A compact home with all the amenities
- Country kitchen combines practicality with access to other areas for eating and entertaining
- Two-way fireplace joins the dining and living areas
- A plant shelf and vaulted ceiling highlight the master bedroom
- 3 bedrooms, 2 1/2 baths, 2-car garage
- Basement foundation

Rear Elevation

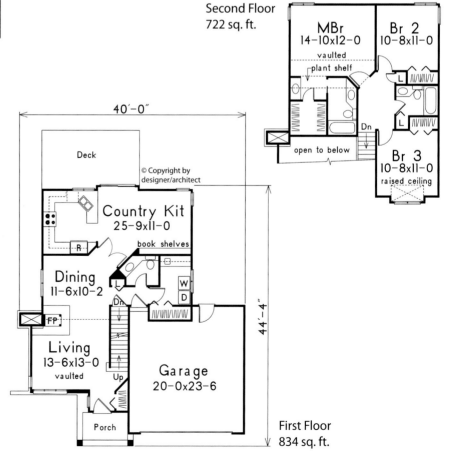

Second Floor
722 sq. ft.

MBr
14-10x12-0
vaulted
plant shelf

Br 2
10-8x11-0

Dn

open to below

Br 3
10-8x11-0
raised ceiling

40'-0"

Deck

© Copyright by
designer/architect

Country Kit
25-9x11-0

book shelves

R

Dining
11-6x10-2

W
D

44'-4"

FP

Living
13-6x13-0
vaulted

Up

Garage
20-0x23-6

Porch

First Floor
834 sq. ft.

Second Floor
592 sq. ft.

attic access
knee space
shelf
linen
step
shelf
36" wall
DN
UP
books

Mstr. Suite
17-8 x 16-4

8'-0" ceiling

slope

Balcony

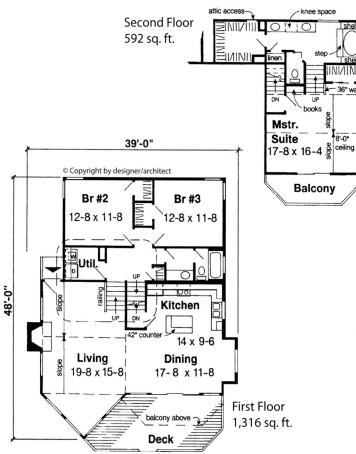

39'-0"

© Copyright by designer/architect

Br #2
12-8 x 11-8

Br #3
12-8 x 11-8

48'-0"

W
D
Util.

slope
railing
UP
UP
DN

Kitchen

42" counter

14 x 9-6

slope

Living
19-8 x 15-8

Dining
17-8 x 11-8

balcony above

Deck

First Floor
1,316 sq. ft.

Rear View

Special features

- 1,375 total square feet of living area
- Den can easily convert to a second bedroom
- A center island in the kitchen allows extra space for organizing and food preparation
- Centrally located laundry room
- 1 bedroom, 2 baths, 2-car rear entry garage
- Basement foundation

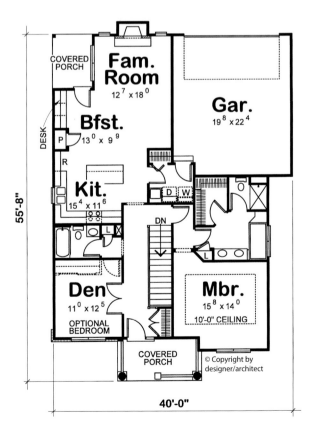

COVERED PORCH

Fam. Room 12⁷ x 18⁰

Gar. 19⁸ x 22⁴

DESK

P

R

Bfst. 13⁰ x 9⁹

Kit. 15⁴ x 11⁶

D W

DN

L

L

Den 11⁰ x 12⁵

OPTIONAL BEDROOM

Mbr. 15⁸ x 14⁰

10'-0" CEILING

COVERED PORCH

55'-8"

40'-0"

First Floor
1,516 sq. ft.

Width: 38'-11"
Depth: 68'-5"

Two Car Garage
22'x 23'6"

Porch

Breakfast

Master Bedroom
15'x 15'4"

Dining
13'6"x 12'

Living
18'x 17'6"

Porch

© Copyright by designer/architect

Second Floor
840 sq. ft.

Bedroom
14'x 11'

Bedroom
15'5"x 12'

Bedroom
14'x 11'6"

Open To Below

Special features

- 2,356 total square feet of living area
- Transoms above front windows create a custom feel to this design
- Spacious master bath has double vanities, toilet closet, and an oversized whirlpool tub
- Covered rear porch off the sunny breakfast area is ideal for grilling or relaxing
- 4 bedrooms, 2 1/2 baths, 2-car side entry garage
- Slab foundation

Special features

- 1,934 total square feet of living area
- The master suite has access onto the covered porch and enjoys a private bath with two walk-in closets
- Extra storage in the garage
- Centralized laundry area
- 3 bedrooms, 2 baths, 2-car rear entry garage
- Crawl space or slab foundation, please specify when ordering

Side View

36'-8"

85'-0"

GARAGE
21'-4" X 20'-0"

STORAGE

GRILLING
PORCH
6'-10" X 10'-2"

MASTER
SUITE
16'-10" X 13'-10"
11" BOXED CEILING

M.B.
10'-8" X 17'-8"

WHP
TUB

BENCH W/
STORAGE

BREAKFAST
NOOK
9'-1" X 6'-10"

PAN

LIN

LAU.
6'-4" X 8'-6"

LIN

KITCHEN
11'-8" X 10'-8"

BEDROOM 2
12'-4" X 13'-2"

COMPUTER
CENTER

LIN

DINING
13'-11" X 11'-0"

8" COLUMNS

BED RM. 3 /
STUDY
12'-6" X 11'-0"

FOYER

GREAT ROOM
15'-8" X 20'-8"

3' GAS
FIREPLACE

11" BOXED CEILING

COVERED
PORCH
15'-4" X 14'-4"

12" COLUMNS

© Copyright by designer/architect

lansandmore.com

First Floor
1,388 sq. ft.

Double Garage
21⁴ x 21⁴

Lnd.
11⁴ x 9⁰

Patio

Brkfst.
11⁸ x 11⁸

Keeping
12⁰ x 14⁸

Screen Porch

Kitchen
15⁶ x 15²

Living
17⁶ x 17⁴

Dining
15⁶ x 11⁶

Foyer

Lav.

Width: 38'-0"
Depth: 79'-0"

© Copyright by designer/architect

Second Floor
1,835 sq. ft.

Bath 3

Excercise / Media / Guest Rm.
16⁰ x 16⁴

Bdrm. 2
11⁴ x 13⁰

Bath 2

Sitting
11⁴ x 8⁸

Bdrm. 3
10⁶ x 12⁶

Master Bdrm.
17⁶ x 17⁸

M. Bath

Special features

- 3,223 total square feet of living area
- The kitchen, breakfast and keeping rooms combine creating an open environment to enjoy
- A screen porch is ideal for outdoor living and has access to the living and keeping rooms
- A built-in computer station on the second floor is the perfect place for children to do schoolwork
- 4 bedrooms, 3 1/2 baths, 2-car rear entry garage
- Basement foundation

Kitchen View

Special features

- 2,320 total square feet of living area
- Energy efficient home with 2" x 6" exterior walls
- Family room is flooded with sunlight from wall of windows
- Decorative columns help separate dining area from living area
- Breakfast nook has sliding glass doors leading to the outdoors
- 4 bedrooms, 2 1/2 baths, 2-car garage
- Crawl space foundation

Second Floor
1,100 sq. ft.

MASTER
12/0 X 14/8

BR. 2
11/4 X 10/0

LINEN

LOFT
10/10 X 9/8

3 CAR VER.
20/4 X 10/0

BR. 4
11/4 X 10/0

DN

LIVING RM
BELOW

BR. 3
10/8 X 10/8

© Copyright by designer/architect

NOOK
11/0 X 8/0 +/-
(9' CLG.)

FAMILY
16/4 X 14/8
(9' CLG.)

DINING
11/2 X 10/0
(9' CLG.)

REF.

50'

GARAGE
19/2 X 22/8
3 CAR - 29/2 X 22/8

VAULTED
LIVING
14/10 X 12/6

UP

DEN
11/0 X 11/2

First Floor
1,220 sq. ft.

◄ 40' ►
3 CAR VER. 49' WIDE

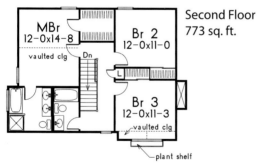

MBr
12-0x14-8

Br 2
12-0x11-0

vaulted clg

Dn

Br 3
12-0x11-3

vaulted clg

plant shelf

Second Floor
773 sq. ft.

36'-0"

46'-8"

Brk fst
10-0x11-0

Kit
9-0x11-7

Dn

Dining
12-0x11-0

Living
15-7x14-4

Up

D | W | P

R

Garage
19-4x20-4

First Floor
802 sq. ft.

Special features

- 1,575 total square feet of living area
- Inviting porch leads to spacious living and dining rooms
- Kitchen with corner windows features an island snack bar, attractive breakfast room bay, convenient laundry area and built-in pantry
- A luxury bath and walk-in closet adorn the master bedroom suite
- 3 bedrooms, 2 1/2 baths, 2-car garage
- Basement foundation, drawings also include crawl space and slab foundations

Rear Elevation

Special features

- 1,699 total square feet of living area
- A double-door entry off the foyer leads to a cozy den that would be ideal as a home office
- At the rear, the kitchen, breakfast and family rooms combine for an easy flow of family activities
- The second floor includes two secondary bedrooms, a handy computer area and an optional expansion area that can be finished as needed
- 3 bedrooms, 2 1/2 baths, 2-car garage
- Basement foundation

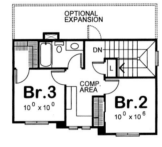

Second Floor
431 sq. ft.

OPTIONAL
EXPANSION

DN

COMP.
AREA

Br.3
10⁰ x 10⁰

Br.2
10⁰ x 10⁶

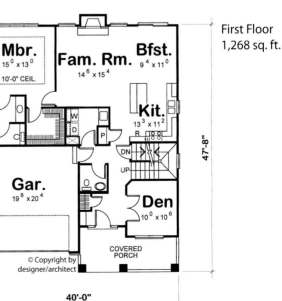

First Floor
1,268 sq. ft.

Mbr.
15⁰ x 13⁰
10'-0" CEIL.

Fam. Rm.
14⁶ x 15⁴

Bfst.
9⁴ x 11⁰

Kit.
13³ x 11²

W
D
P
R

DN
UP

Gar.
19⁸ x 20⁴

Den
10⁰ x 10⁶

47'-8"

© Copyright by
designer/architect

COVERED
PORCH

40'-0"

Special features

- 864 total square feet of living area
- L-shaped kitchen with convenient pantry is adjacent to the dining area
- Easy access to laundry area, linen closet and storage closet
- Both bedrooms include ample closet space
- 2 bedrooms, 1 bath
- Crawl space foundation, drawings also include basement and slab foundations

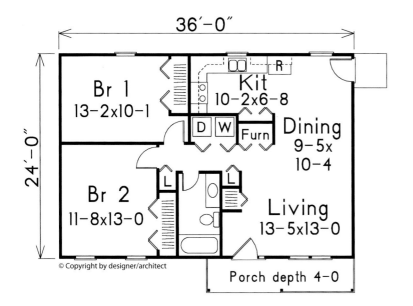

36'-0"

24'-0"

Br 1
13-2x10-1

Kit
10-2x6-8

D W Furn

Dining
9-5x
10-4

Br 2
11-8x13-0

Living
13-5x13-0

© Copyright by designer/architect

Porch depth 4-0

Rear Elevation

Special features

- 1,161 total square feet of living area
- Brickwork and feature window add elegance to this home for a narrow lot
- Living room enjoys a vaulted ceiling, fireplace and opens to the kitchen
- U-shaped kitchen offers a breakfast area with bay window, snack bar and built-in pantry
- 3 bedrooms, 2 baths
- Basement foundation

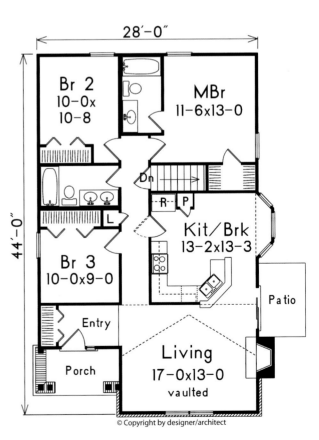

28'-0"

44'-0"

Br 2
10-0x
10-8

MBr
11-6x13-0

Dn

R- P

Kit/Brk
13-2x13-3

Br 3
10-0x9-0

Entry

Patio

Living
17-0x13-0
vaulted

Porch

© Copyright by designer/architect

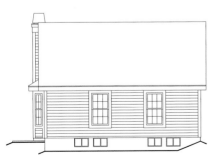

Rear Elevation

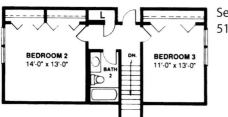

Second Floor
519 sq. ft.

BEDROOM 2
14'-0" x 13'-0"

BATH 2

DN.

BEDROOM 3
11'-0" x 13'-0"

36'-6"

First Floor
1,403 sq. ft.

47'-0"

MASTER BEDROOM
14'-0" x 14'-6"

CLOSET

NOOK
11'-0" x 8'-6"

D.

W.

W.

MASTER BATH
10'-0" x 11'-6"

L

P.R.

P

KITCHEN
11'-0" x 13'-0"

D.W.

REF.

LIVING ROOM
14'-0" x 17'-0"

UP

DINING ROOM
11'-0" x 14'-0"

FOYER

© Copyright by
designer/architect

Special features

- 1,922 total square feet of living area
- Master bedroom includes many luxuries such as an oversized private bath and large walk-in closet
- The kitchen is spacious with a functional eat-in breakfast bar and is adjacent to the nook which is ideal as a breakfast room
- Plenty of storage is featured in both bedrooms on the second floor and in the hall
- Enormous utility room is centrally located on the first floor
- 3 bedrooms, 2 1/2 baths
- Basement foundation

Special features

- 1,143 total square feet of living area
- Enormous stone fireplace in the family room adds warmth and character
- Spacious kitchen with breakfast bar overlooks the family room
- Separate dining area is great for entertaining
- Vaulted family room and kitchen create an open atmosphere
- 2" x 6" exterior walls available, please order plan #598-058D-0075
- 2 bedrooms, 1 bath
- Crawl space foundation

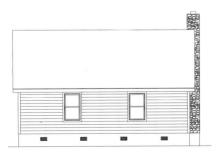

Rear Elevation

34'-0"

38'-0"

Br 1
12-4x12-6

Br 2
12-5x11-0

Family
20-6x16-6

Vaulted Clg

Plant Shelf

D W

F

Kit
12-6x9-6

R

Covered Porch depth 8-0

Dining
13-4x9-0

© Copyright by designer/architect

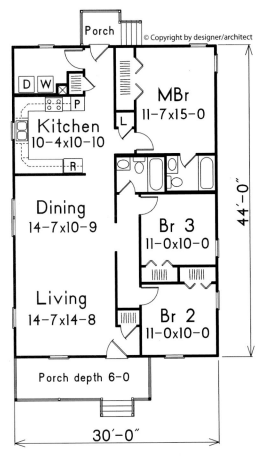

Porch

© Copyright by designer/architect

D | W

Kitchen
10-4x10-10

P

R

MBr
11-7x15-0

L

Dining
14-7x10-9

Br 3
11-0x10-0

Living
14-7x14-8

Br 2
11-0x10-0

44'-0"

Porch depth 6-0

30'-0"

Special features

- 1,320 total square feet of living area
- Functional U-shaped kitchen features a pantry
- Large living and dining areas join to create an open atmosphere
- Secluded master bedroom includes a private full bath
- Covered front porch opens into a large living area with a convenient coat closet
- Utility/laundry room is located near the kitchen
- 3 bedrooms, 2 baths
- Crawl space foundation

Rear Elevation

Special features

- 1,246 total square feet of living area
- Corner living room window adds openness and light
- Out-of-the-way kitchen with dining area accesses the outdoors
- Private first floor master bedroom has a corner window
- Large walk-in closet is located in bedroom #3
- Easily built perimeter allows economical construction
- 3 bedrooms, 2 baths, 2-car garage
- Basement foundation

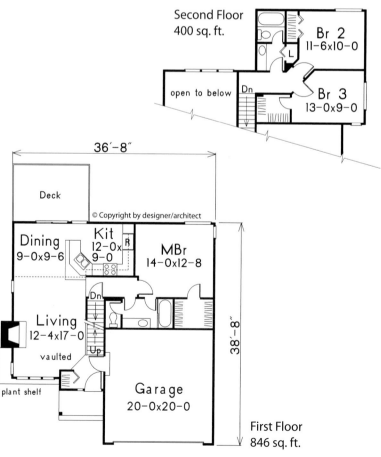

Second Floor
400 sq. ft.

Br 2
11-6x10-0

open to below   Dn

Br 3
13-0x9-0

36'-8"

Deck

© Copyright by designer/architect

Dining
9-0x9-6

Kit
12-0x
9-0

MBr
14-0x12-8

Dn

Living
12-4x17-0

Up

vaulted

plant shelf

Garage
20-0x20-0

38'-8"

First Floor
846 sq. ft.

Rear Elevation

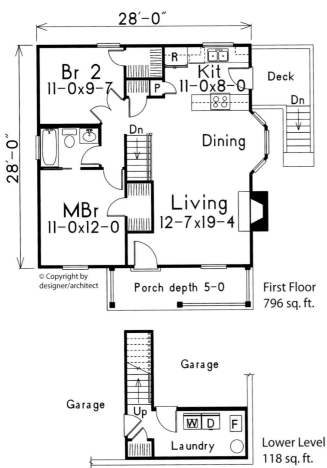

28'-0"

Br 2
11-0x9-7

Kit
11-0x8-0

Deck

Dn

28'-0"

MBr
11-0x12-0

Dining

Living
12-7x19-4

Dn

R

P

© Copyright by
designer/architect

Porch depth 5-0

First Floor
796 sq. ft.

Garage

Garage

Up

W D F

Laundry

Lower Level
118 sq. ft.

Special features

- 914 total square feet of living area
- Large porch for leisure evenings
- Dining area with bay window, open stair and pass-through kitchen create openness
- Basement includes generous garage space, storage area, finished laundry and mechanical room
- 2 bedrooms, 1 bath, 2-car drive under rear entry garage
- Basement foundation

Rear Elevation

Special features

- 1,000 total square feet of living area
- Bath includes convenient closeted laundry area
- Master bedroom includes double closets and private access to the bath
- The foyer features a handy coat closet
- L-shaped kitchen provides easy access outdoors
- 3 bedrooms, 1 bath
- Crawl space foundation, drawings also include basement and slab foundations

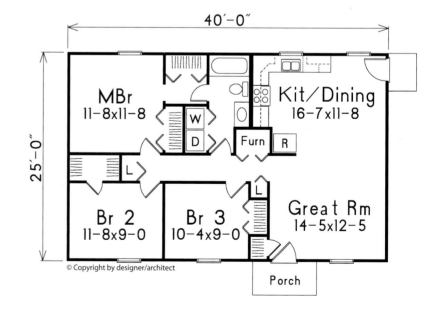

40'-0"

25'-0"

MBr
11-8x11-8

Kit/Dining
16-7x11-8

W

D

Furn

R

L

Br 2
11-8x9-0

Br 3
10-4x9-0

L

Great Rm
14-5x12-5

© Copyright by designer/architect

Porch

Rear Elevation

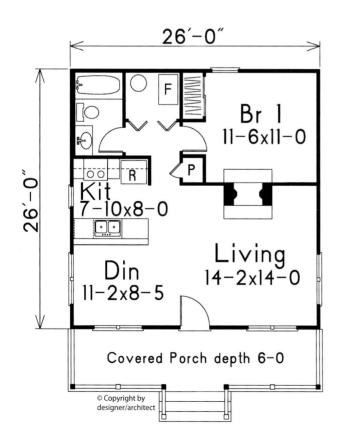

26′-0″

26′-0″

Br 1
11-6x11-0

F

Kit
7-10x8-0

R

P

Living
14-2x14-0

Din
11-2x8-5

Covered Porch depth 6-0

© Copyright by
designer/architect

Special features

- 676 total square feet of living area
- See-through fireplace between bedroom and living area adds character
- Combined dining and living areas create an open feeling
- Full-length front covered porch is perfect for enjoying the outdoors
- Additional storage is available in the utility room
- 2" x 6" exterior walls available, please order plan #598-058D-0074
- 1 bedroom, 1 bath
- Crawl space foundation

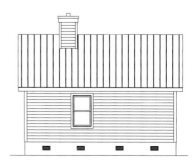

Rear Elevation

Special features

- 1,452 total square feet of living area
- Large living room features a cozy corner fireplace, bayed dining area and access from the entry with guest closet
- Forward master bedroom enjoys having its own bath and linen closet
- Three additional bedrooms share a bath with a double-bowl vanity
- 4 bedrooms, 2 baths
- Basement foundation

Rear Elevation

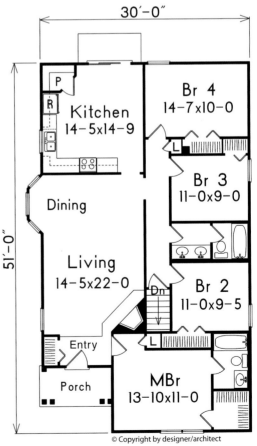

30'-0"

51'-0"

P
R
Kitchen
14-5x14-9

Br 4
14-7x10-0

L

Dining

Br 3
11-0x9-0

Living
14-5x22-0

Dn

Br 2
11-0x9-5

L

Entry

MBr
13-10x11-0

Porch

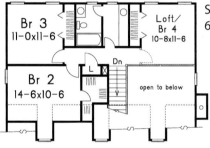

Second Floor
686 sq. ft.

Br 3
11-0x11-6

Loft/
Br 4
10-8x11-6

Br 2
14-6x10-6

Dn

L

open to below

38'-0"

32'-0"

Deck

Brk
8-2x
8-2

Kit
9-4x
13-6

W D

R

Dining
13-6x11-6

Dn

First Floor
1,132 sq. ft.

Living
13-6x15-6

MBr
14-6x13-6

Up

vaulted

Porch depth 6-0

© Copyright by designer/architect

Special features

- 1,818 total square feet of living area
- Breakfast room is tucked behind the kitchen and has a laundry closet and deck access
- Living and dining areas share a vaulted ceiling and fireplace
- Master bedroom has two closets, a large double-bowl vanity and a separate tub and shower
- Large front porch wraps around the home
- 4 bedrooms, 2 1/2 baths, 2-car drive under garage
- Basement foundation

Rear Elevation

Special features

- 1,154 total square feet of living area
- U-shaped kitchen features a large breakfast bar and handy laundry area
- Private second floor bedrooms share a half bath
- Large living/dining area opens to deck
- 3 bedrooms, 1 1/2 baths
- Crawl space foundation, drawings also include slab foundation

Rear Elevation

24´-0″

Br 1
11-11x12-9

Kit
13-5x8-9

D
W
R

Up

Porch

Living/Dining
23-5x12-9

30´-0″

Deck

© Copyright by designer/architect

First Floor
720 sq. ft.

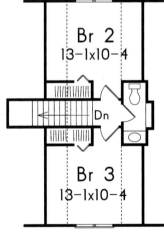

Br 2
13-1x10-4

Dn

Br 3
13-1x10-4

Second Floor
434 sq. ft.

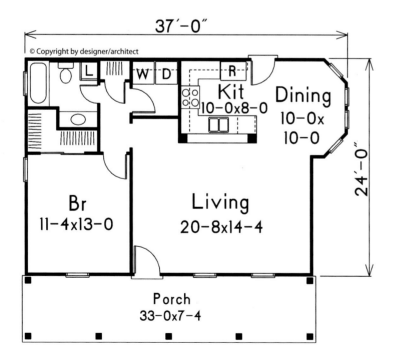

37'-0"

24'-0"

W D

R

L

Kit
10-0x8-0

Dining
10-0x
10-0

Br
11-4x13-0

Living
20-8x14-4

Porch
33-0x7-4

Special features

- 829 total square feet of living area
- U-shaped kitchen opens into living area by a 42" high counter
- Oversized bay window and French door accent dining room
- Gathering space is created by the large living room
- Convenient utility room and linen closet
- 1 bedroom, 1 bath
- Slab foundation

Rear Elevation

Special features

- 1,985 total square feet of living area
- Charming design for a narrow lot
- Dramatic sunken great room features a vaulted ceiling, large double-hung windows and transomed patio doors
- Grand master bedroom includes a double-door entry, large closet, elegant bath and patio access
- 4 bedrooms, 3 1/2 baths, 2-car garage
- Basement foundation

Rear Elevation

© Copyright by designer/architect

35'-0"

56'-0"

MBr
17-0x13-10

Deck

Kitchen
11-4x12-0

Great Rm
13-7x18-8
Sunken
vaulted

Dn

Up

Dining
11-4x12-0

Garage
18-4x21-4

First Floor
1,114 sq. ft.

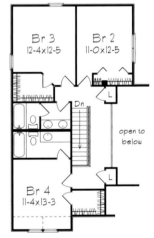

Br 3
12-4x12-5

Br 2
11-0x12-5

open to below

Dn

Br 4
11-4x13-3

Second Floor
871 sq. ft.

Special features

- 800 total square feet of living area
- Master bedroom has a walk-in closet and private access to the bath
- Large living room features a handy coat closet
- Kitchen includes side entrance, closet and convenient laundry area
- 2 bedrooms, 1 bath
- Crawl space foundation, drawings also include basement foundation

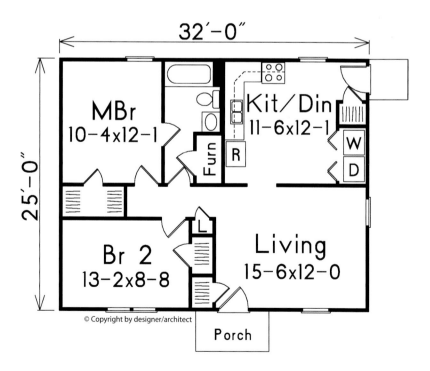

32'-0"

25'-0"

MBr
10-4x12-1

Kit/Din
11-6x12-1

Furn

R

W

D

Br 2
13-2x8-8

Living
15-6x12-0

Porch

© Copyright by designer/architect

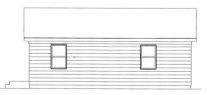

Rear Elevation

Special features

- 864 total square feet of living area
- Large laundry area accesses the outdoors as well as the kitchen
- Front covered porch provides an ideal outdoor living area
- Snack bar in kitchen creates a quick and easy dining area
- 2 bedrooms, 1 bath
- Crawl space or slab foundation, please specify when ordering

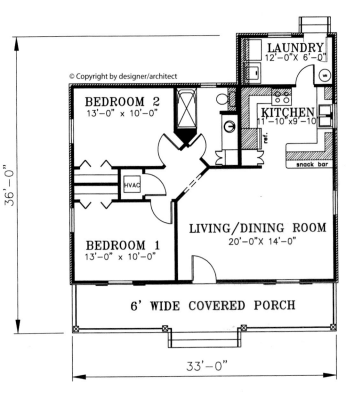

© Copyright by designer/architect

LAUNDRY
12'-0" X 6'-0"

BEDROOM 2
13'-0" x 10'-0"

KITCHEN
11'-10" x 9'-10"

ref.

snack bar

HVAC

BEDROOM 1
13'-0" x 10'-0"

LIVING/DINING ROOM
20'-0" X 14'-0"

36'-0"

6' WIDE COVERED PORCH

33'-0"

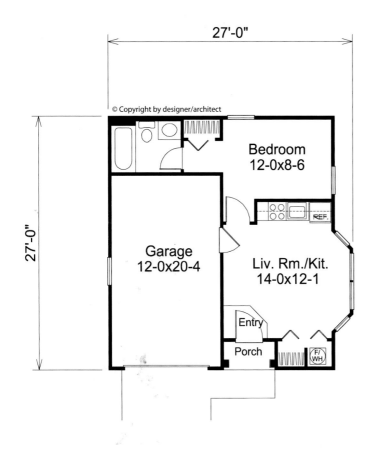

27'-0"

27'-0"

© Copyright by designer/architect

Bedroom
12-0x8-6

Garage
12-0x20-4

Liv. Rm./Kit.
14-0x12-1

REF.

Entry

Porch

F/
WH

Special features

- 421 total square feet of living area
- A recessed porch for protection from inclement weather adds charm to the exterior
- The living room features a large bay window, convenient kitchenette and an entry area with guest closet
- A full size bath and closet are provided for the bedroom
- 1 bedroom, 1 bath, 1-car garage
- Slab foundation

Rear Elevation

Special features

- 1,013 total square feet of living area
- Vaulted ceilings in both the family room and kitchen with dining area just beyond the breakfast bar
- Plant shelf above kitchen is a special feature
- Oversized utility room has space for a full-size washer and dryer
- Hall bath is centrally located with easy access from both bedrooms
- 2" x 6" exterior walls available, please order plan #598-058D-0073
- 2 bedrooms, 1 bath
- Slab foundation

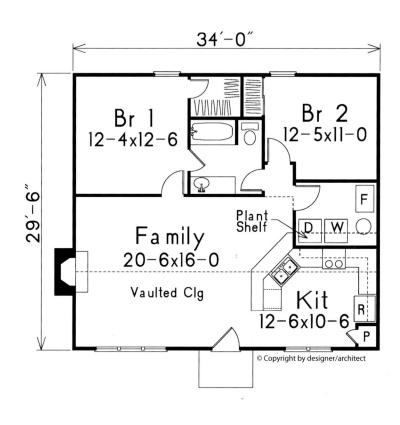

34'-0"

29'-6"

Br 1
12-4x12-6

Br 2
12-5x11-0

Plant Shelf

F

D W

Family
20-6x16-0

Vaulted Clg

Kit
12-6x10-6

R

P

© Copyright by designer/architect

Rear Elevation

Second Floor
397 sq. ft.

open to below

plant shelf

MBr below

Dn

Loft / Br 2
19-3x12-0
vaulted

40'-0"

Deck

Great Rm
19-3x18-6
vaulted

Kit/Brk
17-3x
14-0

P R

34'-0"

Up

MBr
13-7x14-7
vaulted

L

Entry

Dn

Porch

First Floor
1,314 sq. ft.

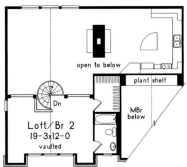

Special features

- 1,711 total square feet of living area
- Entry leads to a vaulted great room, two-story window wall, fireplace, wet bar and balcony
- Bayed breakfast room joins a sun-drenched kitchen and deck
- Vaulted first floor master bedroom features a double-door entry, two closets and bookshelves
- Spiral stairs and a balcony dramatize the loft that doubles as a spacious second bedroom
- 2 bedrooms, 2 1/2 baths
- Basement foundation

Rear View

Special features

- 976 total square feet of living area
- Cozy front porch opens into the large living room
- Convenient half bath is located on the first floor
- All bedrooms are located on the second floor for privacy
- Dining room has access to the outdoors
- 3 bedrooms, 1 1/2 baths
- Basement foundation

Rear Elevation

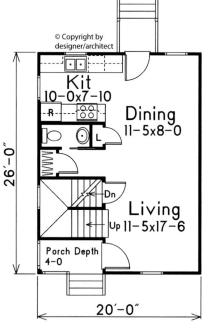

© Copyright by designer/architect

Kit
10-0x7-10

Dining
11-5x8-0

Living
Up 11-5x17-6

Dn

Porch Depth 4-0

26'-0"

20'-0"

First Floor
488 sq. ft.

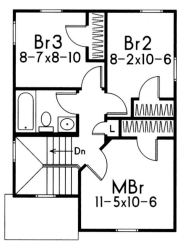

Br3
8-7x8-10

Br2
8-2x10-6

L

Dn

MBr
11-5x10-6

Second Floor
488 sq. ft.

Floor Plan

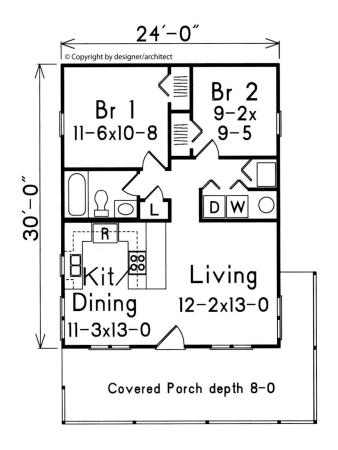

24'-0"

© Copyright by designer/architect

Br 1
11-6x10-8

Br 2
9-2x
9-5

L

D W

R

Kit/
Dining
11-3x13-0

Living
12-2x13-0

30'-0"

Covered Porch depth 8-0

Special features

- 720 total square feet of living area
- Abundant windows in living and dining rooms provide generous sunlight
- Secluded laundry area has a handy storage closet
- U-shaped kitchen with large breakfast bar opens into living area
- Large covered deck offers plenty of outdoor living space
- 2 bedrooms, 1 bath
- Crawl space foundation, drawings also include slab foundation

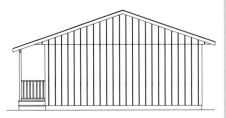

Rear Elevation

Special features

- 828 total square feet of living area
- Vaulted ceiling in living area enhances space
- Convenient laundry room
- Sloped ceiling creates unique style in bedroom #2
- Efficient storage space under the stairs
- Covered entry porch provides a cozy sitting area and plenty of shade
- 2 bedrooms, 1 bath
- Crawl space foundation

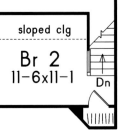

sloped clg

Br 2
11-6x11-1

Dn

Second Floor
168 sq. ft.

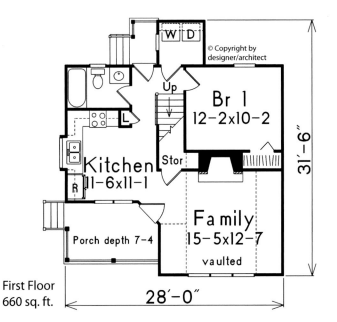

W D

© Copyright by designer/architect

Up

Br 1
12-2x10-2

L

Stor

Kitchen
11-6x11-1

R

31'-6"

Family
15-5x12-7

vaulted

Porch depth 7-4

First Floor
660 sq. ft.

28'-0"

Rear Elevation

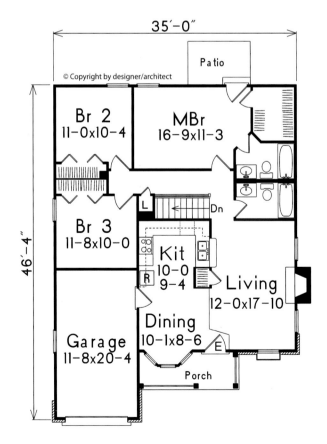

35'-0"

Patio

© Copyright by designer/architect

Br 2
11-0x10-4

MBr
16-9x11-3

Br 3
11-8x10-0

L

Dn

46'-4"

Kit
10-0
9-4

R

Living
12-0x17-10

Dining
10-1x8-6

Garage
11-8x20-4

E

Porch

Special features

- 1,169 total square feet of living area
- Front facade features a distinctive country appeal
- Living room enjoys a wood-burning fireplace and pass-through to the kitchen
- A stylish U-shaped kitchen offers an abundance of cabinet and counterspace with view to the living room
- A large walk-in closet, access to rear patio and private bath are many features of the master bedroom
- 3 bedrooms, 2 baths, 1-car garage
- Basement foundation

Rear Elevation

Special features

- 768 total square feet of living area
- Great room has an attractive box window for enjoying views
- The compact, yet efficient kitchen is open to the great room
- Six closets provide great storage for a compact plan
- Plans include optional third bedroom with an additional 288 square feet of living area
- 2 bedrooms, 1 bath
- Basement foundation, drawings also include crawl space and slab foundations

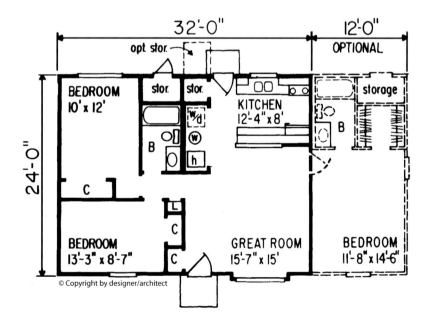

© Copyright by designer/architect

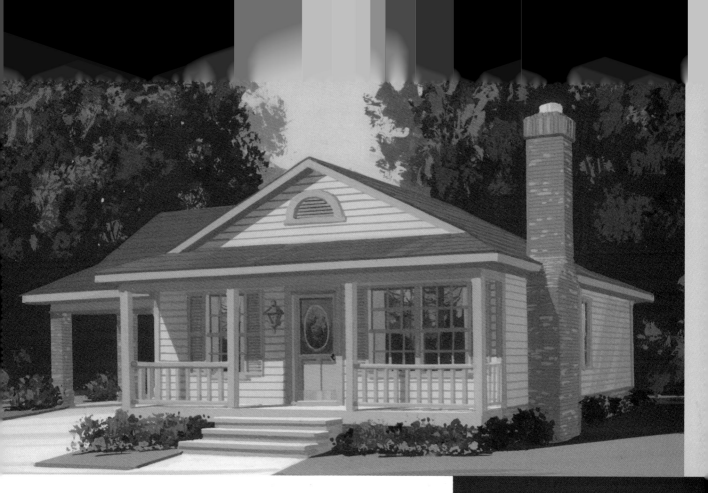

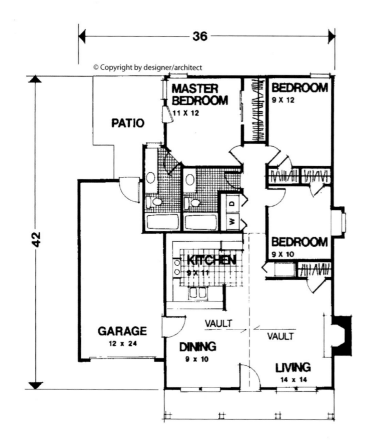

© Copyright by designer/architect

36

42

MASTER BEDROOM
11 X 12

PATIO

BEDROOM
9 X 12

BEDROOM
9 X 10

KITCHEN
9 X 11

GARAGE
12 x 24

DINING
9 x 10

VAULT

VAULT

LIVING
14 x 14

W D

Special features

- 1,050 total square feet of living area
- Master bedroom has its own private bath and access to the outdoors onto a private patio
- Vaulted ceilings in the living and dining areas create a feeling of spaciousness
- The laundry closet is convenient to all bedrooms
- Efficient U-shaped kitchen
- 3 bedrooms, 2 baths, 1-car garage
- Basement or slab foundation, please specify when ordering

Special features

- 1,084 total square feet of living area
- Delightful country porch for quiet evenings
- The living room offers a front feature window which invites the sun and includes a fireplace and dining area with private patio
- The U-shaped kitchen features lots of cabinets and a bayed breakfast room with built-in pantry
- Both bedrooms have walk-in closets and access to their own bath
- 2 bedrooms, 2 baths
- Basement foundation

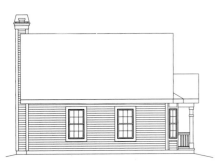

Rear Elevation

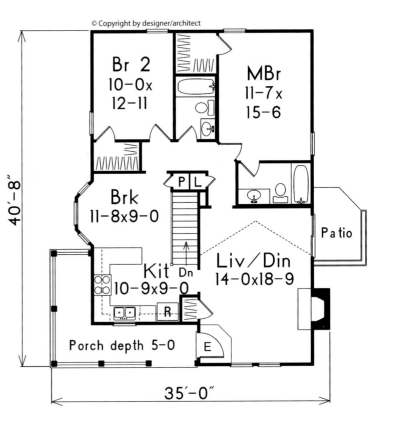

Br 2
10-0x 12-11

MBr
11-7 x 15-6

Brk
11-8x9-0

P | L

Kit
10-9x9-0   Dn

Liv/Din
14-0x18-9

Patio

R

E

Porch depth 5-0

40'-8"

35'-0"

Special features

- 1,230 total square feet of living area
- Spacious living room accesses the huge deck
- Bedroom #3 features a balcony overlooking the deck
- Kitchen with dining area accesses the outdoors
- Washer and dryer are tucked under the stairs for space efficiency
- 3 bedrooms, 1 bath
- Crawl space foundation, drawings also include slab foundation

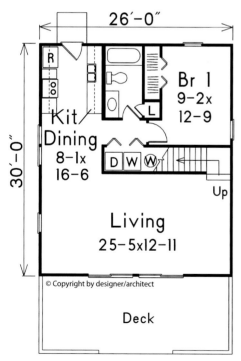

26´-0"

30´-0"

R

Kit

Dining
8-1x
16-6

D W W

Br 1
9-2x
12-9

L

Up

Living
25-5x12-11

© Copyright by designer/architect

Deck

First Floor
780 sq. ft.

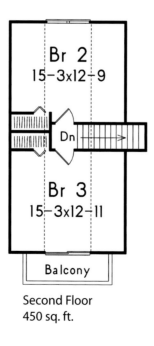

Br 2
15-3x12-9

Dn

Br 3
15-3x12-11

Balcony

Second Floor
450 sq. ft.

Rear Elevation

Special features

- 1,836 total square feet of living area
- Foyer sparkles with spiral stair, a sloped ceiling and celestial windows
- Living room enjoys fireplace with bookshelves and view to the outdoors
- U-shaped kitchen includes eat-in breakfast area and dining nearby
- Master bedroom revels in having a balcony overlooking the living room, a large walk-in closet and private bath
- 3 bedrooms, 2 1/2 baths
- Crawl space foundation, drawings also include slab foundation

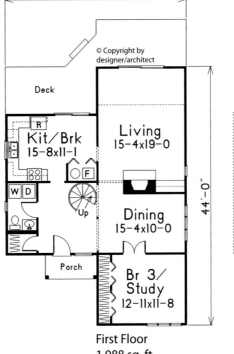

First Floor
1,088 sq. ft.

32'-0"

© Copyright by designer/architect

Deck

Kit/Brk
15-8x11-1

W D

Living
15-4x19-0

F

Up

Dining
15-4x10-0

Porch

Br 3/
Study
12-11x11-8

44'-0"

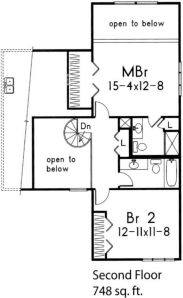

Second Floor
748 sq. ft.

open to below

MBr
15-4x12-8

Dn

L
L

open to below

Br 2
12-11x11-8

Special features

- 1,464 total square feet of living area
- Energy efficient home with 2" x 6" exterior walls
- Contemporary styled home has a breathtaking two-story foyer and a lovely open staircase
- U-shaped kitchen is designed for efficiency
- Elegant great room has a cozy fireplace
- 3 bedrooms, 2 1/2 baths, 2-car garage
- Crawl space foundation

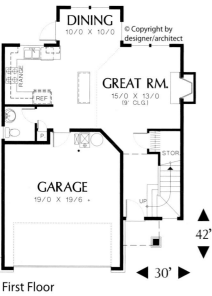

DINING
10/0 X 10/0

© Copyright by designer/architect

GREAT RM.
15/0 X 13/0
(9' CLG.)

RANGE

REF

STOR

GARAGE
19/0 X 19/6 +

UP

42'

30'

First Floor
655 sq. ft.

MASTER
12/0 X 13/0

LINEN

BR. 3
10/8 X 10/0

DN

FOYER BELOW

BR. 2
11/0 X 11/8

Second Floor
809 sq. ft.

Special features

- 2,050 total square feet of living area
- Large kitchen and dining area have access to garage and porch
- Master bedroom features a unique turret design, private bath and large walk-in closet
- Laundry facilities are conveniently located near the bedrooms
- 2" x 6" exterior walls available, please order plan #598-001D-0112
- 3 bedrooms, 2 1/2 baths, 2-car side entry garage
- Basement foundation, drawings also include crawl space and slab foundations

Rear Elevation

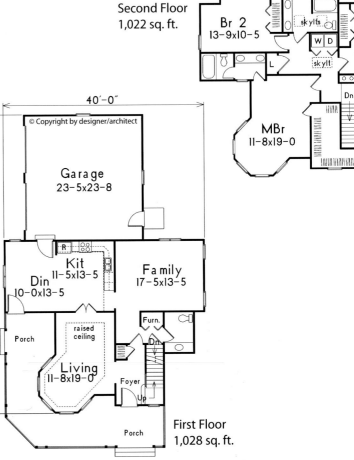

Second Floor
1,022 sq. ft.

Br 2
13-9x10-5

Br 3
9-4x
13-5

W D

skylts

sk ylt

L

MBr
11-8x19-0

Dn

40'-0"

© Copyright by designer/architect

57'-4"

Garage
23-5x23-8

Kit
11-5x13-5

Din
10-0x13-5

Family
17-5x13-5

R

Furn.

raised ceiling

Porch

Dn

Living
11-8x19-0

Foyer

Up

Porch

First Floor
1,028 sq. ft.

Special features

- 1,092 total square feet of living area
- A box window and inviting porch with dormers create a charming facade
- Eat-in kitchen offers a pass-through breakfast bar, corner window wall to patio, pantry and convenient laundry room with half bath
- Master bedroom features a double-door entry and walk-in closet
- 3 bedrooms, 1 1/2 baths, 1-car garage
- Basement foundation

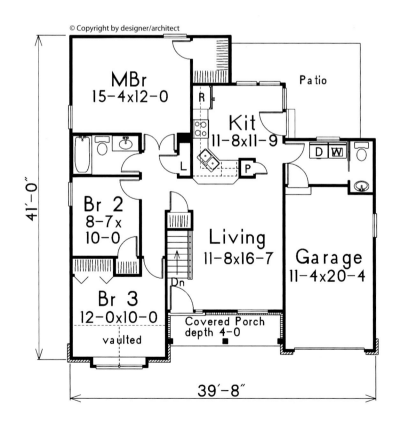

© Copyright by designer/architect

MBr
15-4x12-0

Patio

Kit
11-8x11-9

R F

L

P

D W

Br 2
8-7x
10-0

Living
11-8x16-7

Garage
11-4x20-4

Dn

Br 3
12-0x10-0
vaulted

Covered Porch
depth 4-0

41'-0"

39'-8"

Rear Elevation

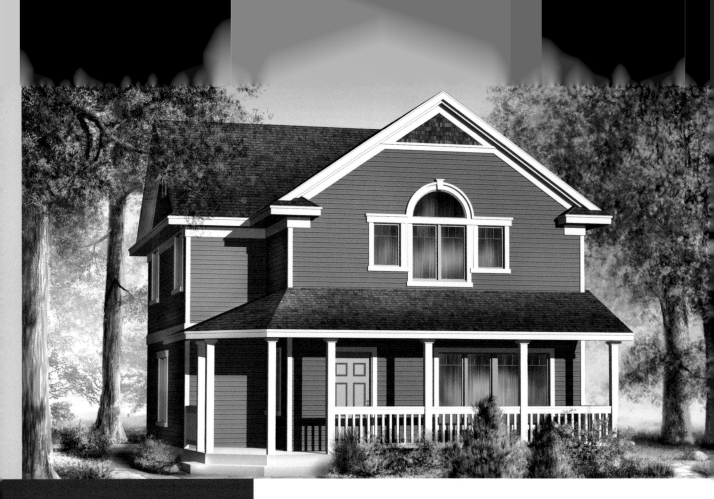

Special features

- 1,649 total square feet of living area
- Energy efficient home with 2" x 6" exterior walls
- Ideal design for a narrow lot
- Country kitchen includes an island and eating bar
- Master bedroom has a 12' vaulted ceiling and a charming arched window
- 4 bedrooms, 2 1/2 baths, 2-car side entry garage
- Basement or crawl space foundation, please specify when ordering

Width: 30'-0"
Depth: 52'-0"

© Copyright by designer/architect

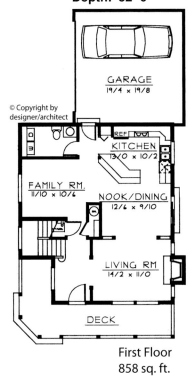

GARAGE
19/4 x 19/8

KITCHEN
13/0 x 10/2

REF

FAMILY RM.
11/10 x 10/6

NOOK/DINING
12/6 x 9/10

LIVING RM.
14/2 x 11/0

DECK

First Floor
858 sq. ft.

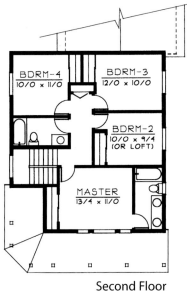

BDRM-4
10/0 x 11/0

BDRM-3
12/0 x 10/0

BDRM-2
10/0 x 9/4
(OR LOFT)

MASTER
13/4 x 11/0

Second Floor
791 sq. ft.

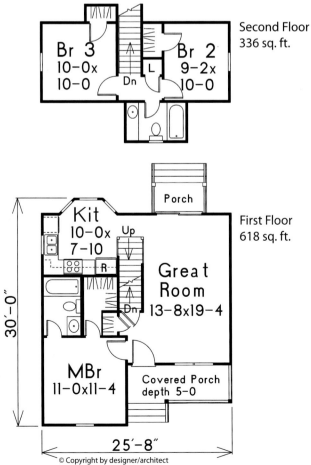

Br 3
10-0x
10-0

Dn

L

Br 2
9-2x
10-0

Second Floor
336 sq. ft.

Porch

Kit
10-0x
7-10

Up

R

Great
Room
13-8x19-4

Dn

MBr
11-0x11-4

Covered Porch
depth 5-0

First Floor
618 sq. ft.

30'-0"

25'-8"

Special features

- 954 total square feet of living area
- Kitchen has a cozy bayed eating area
- Master bedroom has a walk-in closet and private bath
- Large great room has access to the back porch
- Convenient coat closet is near the front entry
- 3 bedrooms, 2 baths
- Basement foundation

Rear Elevation

Special features

- 1,366 total square feet of living area
- Energy efficient home with 2" x 6" exterior walls
- A delightful front porch opens into the roomy living area, perfect for family gatherings
- The kitchen features a wrap-around counter connecting to the dining room that enjoys access to the backyard
- Relax in the master bedroom suite that offers a private bath, dressing area and walk-in closet
- 2 bedrooms, 2 baths, 2-car garage
- Basement foundation

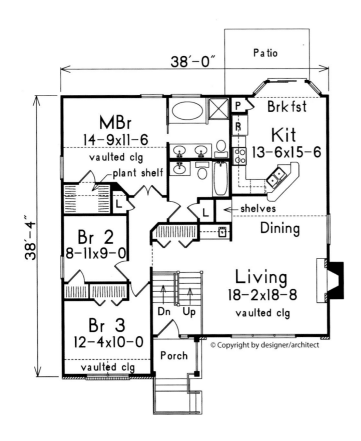

38'-0"

Patio

MBr
14-9x11-6
vaulted clg

plant shelf

L

Br 2
8-11x9-0

Br 3
12-4x10-0
vaulted clg

Porch

Dn   Up

P

R

Brkfst

Kit
13-6x15-6

shelves

L

Dining

Living
18-2x18-8
vaulted clg

38'-4"

© Copyright by designer/architect

Special features

- 1,340 total square feet of living area
- Grand-sized vaulted living and dining rooms offer fireplace, wet bar and breakfast counter open to a spacious kitchen
- Vaulted master bedroom features a double-door entry, walk-in closet and an elegant bath
- Basement includes a huge two-car garage and space for a bedroom/ bath expansion
- 3 bedrooms, 2 baths, 2-car drive under garage with storage area
- Basement foundation

Rear Elevation

Special features

- 1,409 total square feet of living area
- A trio of decorative dormers and a wide covered front porch give this charming one-story cottage a country flavor
- The spacious living room with its cozy fireplace leads into the dining room easily served by an efficient kitchen
- The deluxe master suite has a cathedral ceiling, sliding glass doors to a private terrace, a large walk-in closet and a private bath with whirlpool tub
- 3 bedrooms, 2 baths, optional 2-car garage
- Slab, crawl space or basement foundation, please specify when ordering

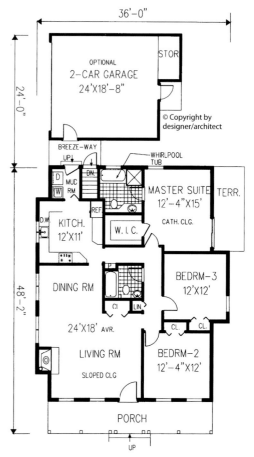

36'–0"

24'–0"

48'–2"

OPTIONAL
2-CAR GARAGE
24'X18'–8"

STOR

© Copyright by designer/architect

BREEZE–WAY
UP
DN

D
W
MUD RM
REF

WHIRLPOOL TUB

MASTER SUITE
12'–4"X15"
CATH. CLG.

TERR.

D.W.
KITCH.
12'X11'
W. I. C.

DINING RM

24'X18' AVR.

LIVING RM
SLOPED CLG

CL.
LIN
BEDRM-3
12'X12'

CL.
CL.
BEDRM-2
12'–4"X12'

PORCH

UP

Special features

- 994 total square feet of living area
- Energy efficient home with 2" x 6" exterior walls
- Beautiful and sunny dining area
- Kitchen has center island ideal for food preparation as well as additional dining
- Plenty of closets and storage throughout
- 2 bedrooms, 1 bath
- Basement foundation

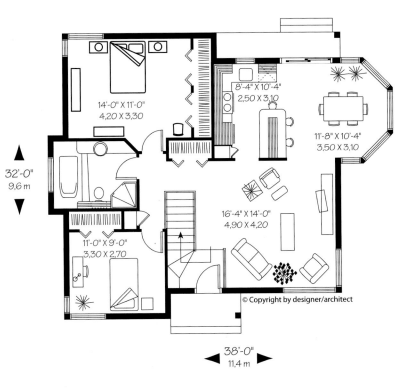

14'-0" X 11'-0"
4,20 X 3,30

8'-4" X 10'-4"
2,50 X 3,10

11'-8" X 10'-4"
3,50 X 3,10

32'-0"
9,6 m

11'-0" X 9'-0"
3,30 X 2,70

16'-4" X 14'-0"
4,90 X 4,20

38'-0"
11,4 m

Special features

- 929 total square feet of living area
- Spacious living room with dining area has access to 8' x 12' deck through glass sliding doors
- Splendid U-shaped kitchen features a breakfast bar, oval window above sink and impressive cabinet storage
- Master bedroom enjoys a walk-in closet and large elliptical window
- Laundry and storage closet are located off the first floor garage
- 2 bedrooms, 1 bath, 3-car side entry garage
- Slab foundation

Rear Elevation

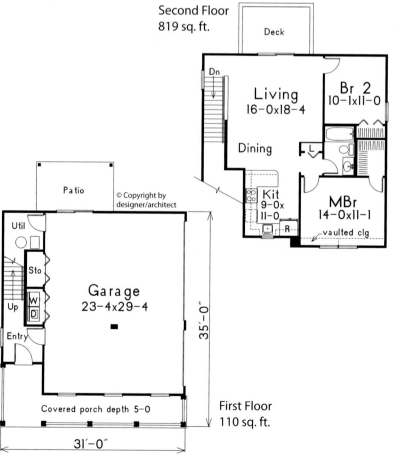

Second Floor
819 sq. ft.

Deck

Dn

Living
16-0x18-4

Br 2
10-1x11-0

Dining

L

Kit
9-0x
11-0

MBr
14-0x11-1

R

vaulted clg

© Copyright by designer/architect

Patio

Util

Sto

Up

W D

Entry

Garage
23-4x29-4

35'-0"

Covered porch depth 5-0

First Floor
110 sq. ft.

31'-0"

First Floor
1,368 sq. ft.

© Copyright by designer/architect

Screened Porch
36-0 x 8-0

Kitchen
11-6 x 13-0
Raised Bar
Island
Ref.

W D
Utility
6-2 x 7-4
Cabinets

Mstr. Closet
7-0 x 9-8

Dining
10-0 x 11-6
(Clear)
9' Clg. Ht.

Computer Center
8' Clg. Ht.
Up
Up
Pan.
1/2 Bath

Mstr. Bath
Shwr.
Linen
L
Jet Tub

Great Room
19-6 x 19-8
(Clear)
9' Clg. Ht.
Gas Logs

Master Bedroom
15-6 x 15-6
9' Clg. Ht.

Covered Porch
36-0 x 6-0

Width: 38'-0"
Depth: 52'-0"

Second Floor
532 sq. ft.

Bedroom 2
10-6 x 13-0
(Clear)
8' Clg. Ht.

Down
Hall
Down
Attic Access

Tub/Shwr.
Bath 2
9-0 x 6-4

Bedroom 3
10-6 x 12-10
8' Clg. Ht.

- 1,900 total square feet of living area
- Plenty of outdoor living space is provided with this home thanks to the large covered porch spanning the front of the home and the large screened porch that spans the rear
- A hallway computer center on the first floor is located in a convenient spot, just adjacent to the large and spacious great room
- The spacious master bedroom has an enormous walk-in closet and a private bath
- 3 bedrooms, 2 1/2 baths, optional 2-car carport
- Slab or crawl space foundation, please specify when ordering

Special features

- 1,604 total square feet of living area
- Energy efficient home with 2" x 6" exterior walls
- Ideal design for a narrow lot
- Living and dining areas combine for a spacious feel
- Secluded study has a double-door entry for privacy
- Master bedroom has a spacious private bath
- 3 bedrooms, 2 baths, 2-car garage
- Slab foundation

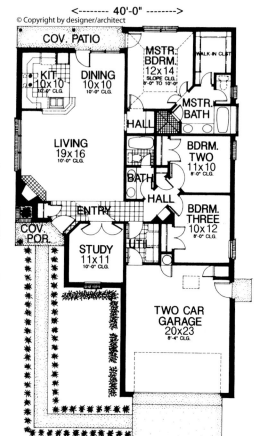

© Copyright by designer/architect

<-------- 40'-0" -------->

COV. PATIO

KIT
10 x 10
10'-0" CLG.

DINING
10 x 10
10'-0" CLG.

MSTR.
BDRM.
12 x 14
SLOPE CLG.
8'-0" TO 10'-0"

WALK-IN CLST.

MSTR.
BATH

HALL

LIVING
19 x 16
10'-0" CLG.

BDRM.
TWO
11 x 10
8'-0" CLG.

BATH

HALL

BDRM.
THREE
10 x 12
8'-0" CLG.

ENTRY

COV.
POR.

STUDY
11 x 11
10'-0" CLG.

UTIL

65'-10"

TWO CAR
GARAGE
20 x 23
8'-4" CLG.

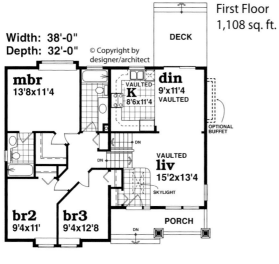

Width: 38'-0"
Depth: 32'-0"

© Copyright by designer/architect

First Floor
1,108 sq. ft.

DECK

mbr
13'8x11'4

VAULTED
K
8'6x11'4

din
9'x11'4
VAULTED

OPTIONAL
BUFFET

DN

VAULTED
liv
15'2x13'4

SKYLIGHT

br2
9'4x11'

br3
9'4x12'8

DN

PORCH

DN

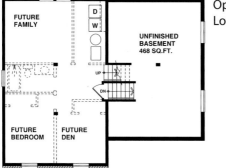

Optional
Lower Level

FUTURE
FAMILY

D
W

UNFINISHED
BASEMENT
468 SQ.FT.

UP

DN

FUTURE
BEDROOM

FUTURE
DEN

Special features

- 1,108 total square feet of living area
- Energy efficient home with 2" x 6" exterior walls
- Master bedroom offers a walk-in closet, a full bath and a box-bay window
- Vaulted ceilings in the kitchen, living and dining rooms make this home appear larger than its actual size
- Compact, but efficient kitchen is U-shaped so everything is within reach
- Optional lower level has an additional 1,108 square feet of living area
- 3 bedrooms, 2 baths
- Partial basement/crawl space or basement foundation, please specify when ordering

Special features

- 632 total square feet of living area
- Porch leads to a vaulted entry and stair with feature window, coat closet and access to garage/laundry
- Cozy living room offers a vaulted ceiling, fireplace, large palladian window and pass-through to kitchen
- A garden tub with arched window is part of a very roomy bath
- 1 bedroom, 1 bath, 2-car garage
- Slab foundation

Rear Elevation

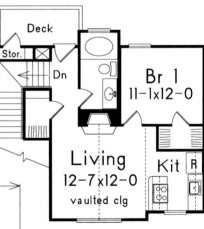

Deck

Stor.

Dn

Br 1
11-1x12-0

Living
12-7x12-0
vaulted clg

Kit

R

Second Floor
512 sq. ft.

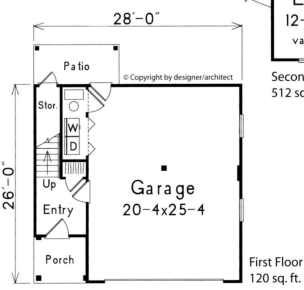

28'-0"

26'-0"

Patio

Stor.

W
D

Up

Entry

Garage
20-4x25-4

Porch

© Copyright by designer/architect

First Floor
120 sq. ft.

655

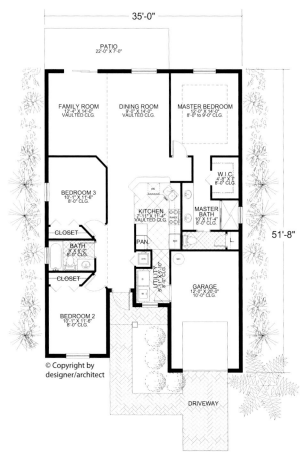

PATIO
22'-0" X 7'-0"

35'-0"

FAMILY ROOM
12'-4" X 14'-0"
VAULTED CLG.

DINING ROOM
9'-0" X 14'-0"
VAULTED CLG.

MASTER BEDROOM
12'-0" X 14'-0"
8'-0" to 9'-0" CLG.

BEDROOM 3
10'-1" X 11'-6"
8'-0" CLG.

W.I.C.
4'-8" X 7'
8'-0" CLG.

KITCHEN
7'-11" X 11'-4"
VAULTED CLG.

MASTER BATH
10' X 11'-4"
8'-0" CLG.

CLOSET

PAN.

BATH
8' X 5'-2"
8'-0" CLG.

51'-8"

CLOSET

UTILITY
5'-1" X 5'-10"
8'-0" CLG.

GARAGE
12'-0" X 20'-0"
10'-0" CLG.

BEDROOM 2
10'-1" X 11'-6"
8'-0" CLG.

© Copyright by
designer/architect

DRIVEWAY

Special features

- 1,382 total square feet of living area
- The family and dining rooms combine for added space and an open atmosphere
- The kitchen is compact, yet designed for efficiency
- The two secondary bedrooms skillfully share a full bath
- Framing - only concrete block available
- 3 bedrooms, 2 baths, 1-car garage
- Slab foundation

Special features

- 1,560 total square feet of living area
- Two-story master bedroom has a sunny dormer above, large walk-in closet and private bath
- Great room has a unique two-story ceiling with dormers
- Spacious kitchen has a large center island creating an ideal workspace
- 3 bedrooms, 2 1/2 baths
- Basement, crawl space or slab foundation, please specify when ordering

Rear View

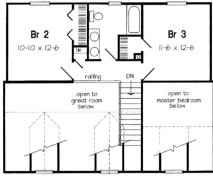

Second Floor
499 sq. ft.

Br 2
10-10 x 12-6

Br 3
11-6 x 12-6

railing   DN

open to great room below

open to master bedroom below

First Floor
1,061 sq. ft.

Optional Deck w/ Hot Tub

privacy fence

Kitchen
8-1 x 12-7

Dining
9-8 x 12-7
8' clg

Island

DW

D

W

stor.

8' clg

DN

Master Br
12 x 14-6
vault clg

17' flat clg

34'-0"

Great Room
19-7 x 14-10
vault clg

UP

flat clg
@15'-7"

© Copyright by designer/architect

Porch

40'-0"

First Floor
1,012 sq. ft.

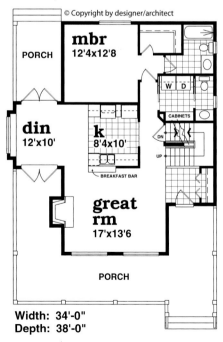

© Copyright by designer/architect

PORCH

mbr
12'4x12'8

W D

CABINETS

din
12'10'

k
8'4x10'

DN

UP

BREAKFAST BAR

great rm
17'x13'6

PORCH

Width: 34'-0"
Depth: 38'-0"

Second Floor
576 sq. ft.

br2
12'4x12'8

br3
10'x10'
OR OPTIONAL LOFT

3'6 RAILING

DN

OPEN TO BELOW

Rear View

Special features

- 1,352 total square feet of living area
- Energy efficient home with 2" x 6" exterior walls
- Combined kitchen, living and dining rooms with skylights and a solar bay, create a beautiful and relaxing space
- Access the expansive rear deck through sliding glass doors off the living room
- The master bedroom is private from living areas and other bedrooms
- 3 bedrooms, 2 baths
- Basement, crawl space or slab foundation, please specify when ordering

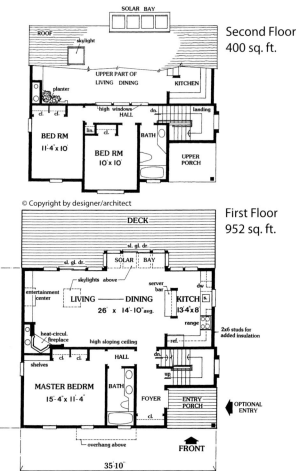

Second Floor
400 sq. ft.

First Floor
952 sq. ft.

© Copyright by designer/architect

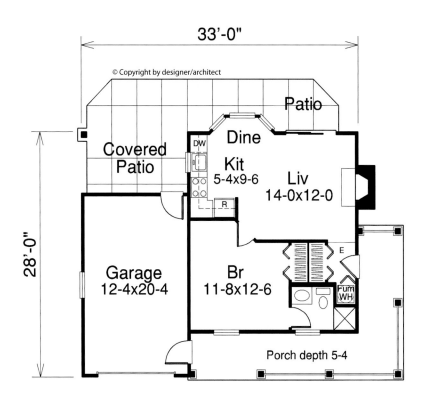

33'-0"

© Copyright by designer/architect

Patio

Covered
Patio

Dine

DW

Kit
5-4x9-6

Liv
14-0x12-0

R

28'-0"

Garage
12-4x20-4

Br
11-8x12-6

E

Furn
WH

Porch depth 5-4

Special features

- 480 total square feet of living area
- Inviting wrap-around porch and rear covered patio are perfect for summer evenings
- Living room features a fireplace, separate entry foyer with coat closet and sliding doors to rear patio
- The compact but complete kitchen includes a dining area with bay window and window at sink for patio views
- 1 bedroom, 1 bath, 1-car garage
- Slab foundation

Rear Elevation

Special features

- 2,030 total square feet of living area
- Energy efficient home with 2" x 6" exterior walls
- Centrally located kitchen serves the formal dining room and bayed breakfast room with ease
- Spacious living room is warmed by a grand fireplace
- The second floor bedrooms are generously sized and each feature built-in desk areas
- 3 bedrooms, 2 1/2 baths
- Basement or crawl space foundation, please specify when ordering

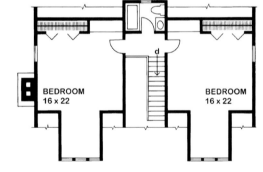

Second Floor
735 sq. ft.

BEDROOM
16 x 22

BEDROOM
16 x 22

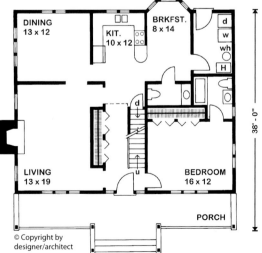

First Floor
1,295 sq. ft.

40' - 0"

38' - 0"

DINING
13 x 12

KIT.
10 x 12

BRKFST.
8 x 14

d
w
wh
H

LIVING
13 x 19

BEDROOM
16 x 12

PORCH

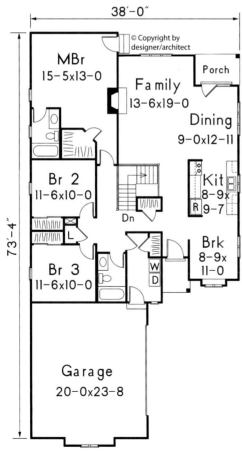

38'-0"

73'-4"

MBr
15-5x13-0

Family
13-6x19-0

Porch

© Copyright by
designer/architect

Dining
9-0x12-11

Br 2
11-6x10-0

Dn

Kit
8-9x
9-7

Brk
8-9x
11-0

W
D

Br 3
11-6x10-0

Garage
20-0x23-8

Special features

- 1,624 total square feet of living area
- Master bedroom has a private entry from the outdoors
- Garage is adjacent to the utility room with convenient storage closet
- Large family and dining areas feature a fireplace and porch access
- Pass-through kitchen opens directly to the cozy breakfast area
- 3 bedrooms, 2 baths, 2-car side entry garage
- Basement foundation, drawings also include crawl space and slab foundations

Rear Elevation

Special features

- 1,266 total square feet of living area
- Energy efficient home with 2" x 6" exterior walls
- Prominent central hall provides a convenient connection for all main rooms
- Design incorporates full-size master bedroom complete with dressing room, bath and walk-in closet
- Angled kitchen includes handy laundry facilities and is adjacent to an oversized storage area
- 3 bedrooms, 2 baths, 2-car rear entry garage
- Crawl space foundation, drawings also include slab foundation

Rear Elevation

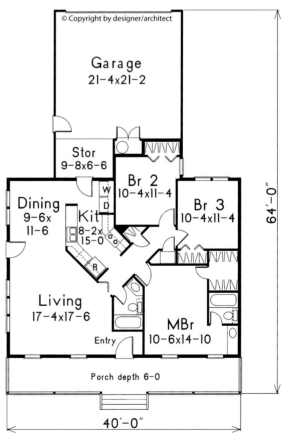

Garage
21-4x21-2

Stor
9-8x6-6

Br 2
10-4x11-4

Br 3
10-4x11-4

Dining
9-6x
11-6

Kit
8-2x
15-0

Living
17-4x17-6

MBr
10-6x14-10

Entry

Porch depth 6-0

64'-0"

40'-0"

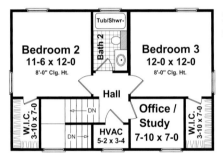

Second Floor
600 sq. ft.

Bedroom 2
11-6 x 12-0
8'-0" Clg. Ht.

Bath 2
Tub/Shwr

Bedroom 3
12-0 x 12-0
8'-0" Clg. Ht.

W.I.C.
3-10 x 7-0

Hall

DN
DN

HVAC
5-2 x 3-4

Office /
Study
7-10 x 7-0

W.I.C.
3-10 x 7-0

© Copyright by designer/architect

First Floor
600 sq. ft.

Covered Or
Screened Porch
9-6 x 5-8

Rear Porch
19-10 x 6-0

Master
Bedroom
11-6 x 12-0
8'-0" Clg. Ht.

Bath
5-0 x 8-4
Tub/Shwr

Kitchen
12-0 x 8-10
P
W/D
DW
Ref.
Raised Bar

W.I.C.
3-10 x 7-10

C

Living Room
17-6 x 10-6
8'-0" Clg. Ht.

UP

Front Porch
30-0x 6-0

Width: 30'-0"
Depth: 32'-0"

Special features

- 1,200 total square feet of living area
- Enjoy the open living area made possible with the raised snack bar connecting the kitchen to the living room
- Front and rear porches provide lovely settings for relaxing in the great outdoors
- Each bedroom features a walk-in closet for easy organization
- Insulated concrete formed exterior walls provide tighter construction, conserving heating and cooling energy
- 3 bedrooms, 2 baths
- Slab or crawl space foundation, please specify when ordering

Special features

- 1,035 total square feet of living area
- Spacious living room is warmed by a stone fireplace and features a bay window with window seat
- Country kitchen opens to the dining room and includes sliding glass doors leading to the patio
- On the second floor, two bedrooms complete the design and share a full bath
- 2 bedrooms, 1 1/2 baths
- Basement and crawl space foundation, please specify when ordering

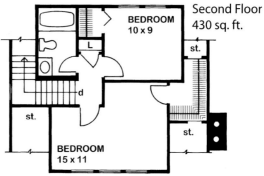

Second Floor
430 sq. ft.

BEDROOM
10 x 9

st.

st.

st.

BEDROOM
15 x 11

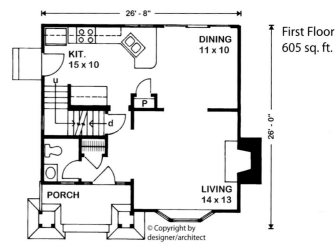

26' - 8"

KIT.
15 x 10

DINING
11 x 10

First Floor
605 sq. ft.

26' - 0"

P

PORCH

LIVING
14 x 13

© Copyright by
designer/architect

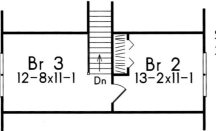

Second Floor
300 sq. ft.

Br 3
12-8x11-1

Dn

Br 2
13-2x11-1

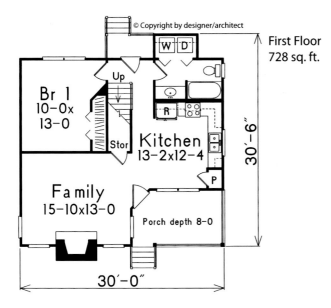

© Copyright by designer/architect

W D

Up

Br 1
10-0x
13-0

Stor

Kitchen
13-2x12-4

R

P

Family
15-10x13-0

Porch depth 8-0

First Floor
728 sq. ft.

30'-6"

30'-0"

Special features

- 1,028 total square feet of living area
- Well-designed bath contains laundry facilities
- L-shaped kitchen has a handy pantry
- Tall windows flank the family room fireplace
- Cozy covered porch provides unique angled entry into home
- 3 bedrooms, 1 bath
- Crawl space foundation

Rear Elevation

Special features

- 2,647 total square feet of living area
- This home has a large laundry room with plenty of counterspace for staying organized
- The bayed breakfast room is a cheerful way to start the day
- The master bedroom has its own private bath with a grand whirlpool tub set into a bay window for added drama
- Framing - only concrete block available
- 5 bedrooms, 3 baths, 2-car garage
- Slab foundation

First Floor
1,338 sq. ft.

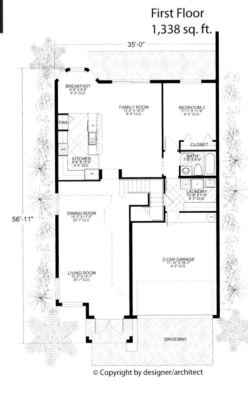

Second Floor
1,309 sq. ft.

© Copyright by designer/architect

Special features

- 1,040 total square feet of living area
- An island in the kitchen greatly simplifies your food preparation efforts
- A wide archway joins the formal living room to the dramatic angled kitchen and dining room
- Optional second floor has an additional 597 square feet of living area
- Optional first floor design has two bedrooms including a large master bedroom that enjoys a private luxury bath
- 3 bedrooms, 1 1/2 baths
- Basement, crawl space or slab foundation, please specify when ordering

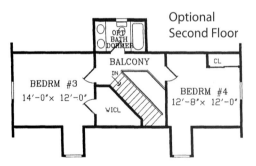

Optional Second Floor

BEDRM #3
14'-0" x 12'-0"

OPT BATH DORMER

BALCONY

BEDRM #4
12'-8" x 12'-0"

WICL

CL

© Copyright by designer/architect

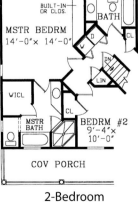

2-Bedroom Option

BUILT-IN OR CLOS.

BATH

MSTR BEDRM
14'-0" x 14'-0"

WICL

CL

MSTR BATH

BEDRM #2
9'-4" x 10'-0"

COV PORCH

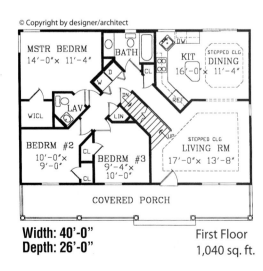

MSTR BEDRM
14'-0" x 11'-0"

BATH

KIT

DINING STEPPED CLG
16'-0" x 11'-4"

WICL

LAV

LIN

BEDRM #2
10'-0" x 9'-0"

CL

BEDRM #3
9'-4" x 10'-0"

CL

LIVING RM STEPPED CLG
17'-0" x 13'-8"

COVERED PORCH

Width: 40'-0"
Depth: 26'-0"

First Floor
1,040 sq. ft.

Special features

- 1,124 total square feet of living area
- Energy efficient home with 2" x 6" exterior walls
- Wrap-around porch creates an outdoor living area
- Large dining area easily accommodates extra guests
- Sunken family room becomes a cozy retreat
- 2 bedrooms, 1 bath, 1-car garage
- Basement foundation

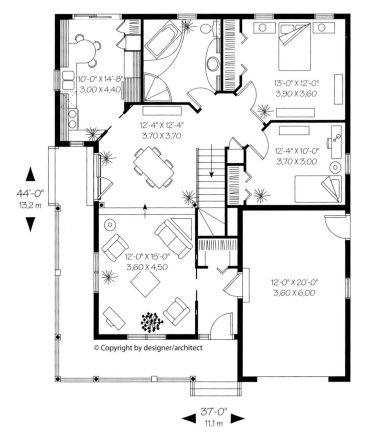

10'-0" X 14'-8"
3,00 X 4,40

13'-0" X 12'-0"
3,90 X 3,60

12'-4" X 12'-4"
3,70 X 3,70

12'-4" X 10'-0"
3,70 X 3,00

44'-0"
13,2 m

12'-0" X 15'-0"
3,60 X 4,50

12'-0" X 20'-0"
3,60 X 6,00

© Copyright by designer/architect

37'-0"
11,1 m

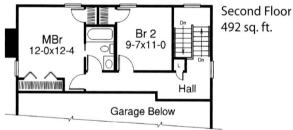

Second Floor
492 sq. ft.

MBr
12-0x12-4

Br 2
9-7x11-0

Dn

Dn

L

Hall

Garage Below

35'-0"

First Floor
513 sq. ft.

Patio

© Copyright by
designer/architect

Din

Living Rm.
18-6x12-8

DW

Kit
8-8x
8-8

Up

R

Up

Entry

W/D

36'-0"

3-Car Garage
34-0x22-4

Special features

- 1,005 total square feet of living area
- Two-story apartment includes a one-story facade featuring triple garage doors and a roof dormer
- Side porch leads to an entry hall which accesses the living room, U-shaped kitchen, powder room and stairs to the second floor
- The large living room has a fireplace, sliding doors to the patio, dining area with bay window and opens to the kitchen with breakfast bar
- 2 bedrooms, 1 1/2 baths, 3-car garage
- Slab foundation

Rear Elevation

Special features

- 1,584 total square feet of living area
- Energy efficient home with 2" x 6" exterior walls
- Kitchen overlooks family room creating a natural gathering place
- Double vanity in master bath
- Dining room flows into living room
- 3 bedrooms, 3 baths, 2-car rear entry garage
- Crawl space foundation

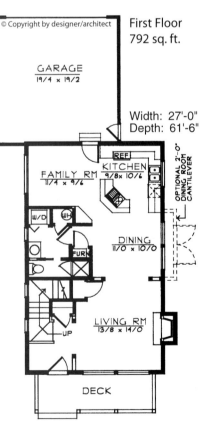

First Floor
792 sq. ft.

GARAGE
19/4 x 19/2

Width: 27'-0"
Depth: 61'-6"

FAMILY RM
11/4 x 9/6

KITCHEN
9/8 x 10/6

REF

OPTIONAL 2'-0"
DINING ROOM
CANTILEVER

W/D   WH

DINING
11/0 x 10/0

FURN

LIVING RM
13/8 x 14/0

UP

DECK

Second Floor
792 sq. ft.

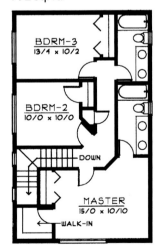

BDRM-3
13/4 x 10/2

BDRM-2
10/0 x 10/0

DOWN

MASTER
15/0 x 10/10

WALK-IN

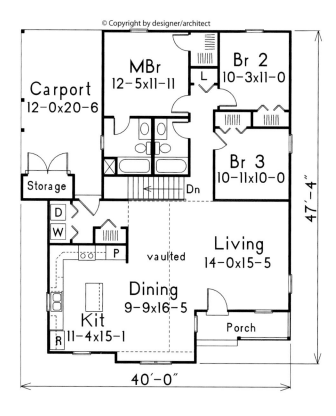

© Copyright by designer/architect

Carport
12-0x20-6

Storage

MBr
12-5x11-11

L

Br 2
10-3x11-0

Br 3
10-11x10-0

Dn

D
W

P

vaulted

Living
14-0x15-5

Dining
9-9x16-5

Kit
11-4x15-1

R

Porch

47'-4"

40'-0"

Special features

- 1,396 total square feet of living area
- Gabled front adds interest to the facade
- Living and dining rooms share a vaulted ceiling
- Master bedroom features a walk-in closet and private bath
- Functional kitchen boasts a center work island and convenient pantry
- 3 bedrooms, 2 baths, 1-car rear entry carport
- Basement foundation, drawings also include crawl space foundation

Rear Elevation

Special features

- 809 total square feet of living area
- This attractive earth berm home is perfectly designed for a vacation retreat
- Nestled in a hillside with only one exposed exterior wall, this home offers efficiency, protection and affordability
- A large porch creates an ideal space for lazy afternoons and quiet evenings
- All rooms are very spacious and three closets plus the laundry room provide abundant storage
- 1 bedroom, 1 bath
- Slab foundation

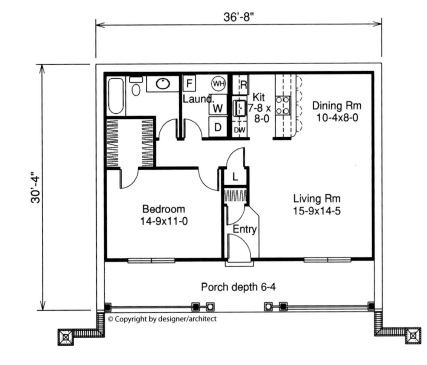

36'-8"

30'-4"

Laund.

F WH R

Kit 7-8 x 8-0

W DW

D

Dining Rm 10-4x8-0

L

Bedroom 14-9x11-0

Living Rm 15-9x14-5

Entry

Porch depth 6-4

© Copyright by designer/architect

Rear Elevation

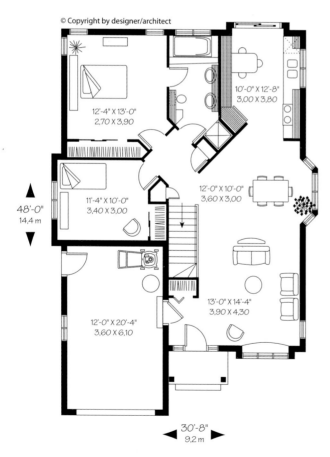

© Copyright by designer/architect

12'-4" X 13'-0"
2,70 X 3,90

10'-0" X 12'-8"
3,00 X 3,80

11'-4" X 10'-0"
3,40 X 3,00

12'-0" X 10'-0"
3,60 X 3,00

48'-0"
14,4 m

13'-0" X 14'-4"
3,90 X 4,30

12'-0" X 20'-4"
3,60 X 6,10

30'-8"
9,2 m

Special features

- 1,103 total square feet of living area
- Energy efficient home with 2" x 6" exterior walls
- All bedrooms are located in one area of the house for privacy
- Bay window enhances dining area
- Living and dining areas combine for a spacious feeling
- Lots of storage throughout
- 2 bedrooms, 1 bath, 1-car garage
- Basement foundation

Special features

- 581 total square feet of living area
- Kitchen/living room features space for dining and spiral steps leading to the loft area
- Large loft area can easily be converted to a bedroom or home office
- Entry space has a unique built-in display niche
- 1 bedroom, 1 bath
- Slab foundation

Rear Elevation

First Floor
449 sq. ft.

Kit/ Living
11-0x17-0
Up

vaulted

Br 1
10-0x10-8

24'-4"

19'-0"

© Copyright by designer/architect

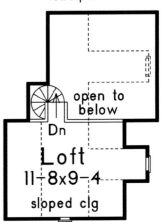

Second Floor
132 sq. ft.

open to below

Dn

Loft
11-8x9-4

sloped clg

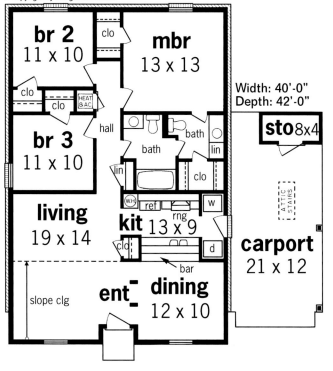

© Copyright by designer/architect

br 2
11 x 10

clo

mbr
13 x 13

clo

clo

HEAT & AC

hall

bath

bath

lin

lin

Width: 40'-0"
Depth: 42'-0"

sto 8x4

br 3
11 x 10

lin

clo

W/H

ref

rng

w

ATTIC STAIRS

living
19 x 14

kit 13 x 9

d

carport
21 x 12

clo

bar

slope clg

ent

dining
12 x 10

- 1,168 total square feet of living area
- Energy efficient home with 2" x 6" exterior walls
- Economical design offers big rooms, ample storage and maximum livability
- The living and dining areas feature a sloped ceiling to add to the spacious feel
- An eating bar between the kitchen and dining area makes serving meals a snap
- 3 bedrooms, 1 1/2 baths, 1-car carport
- Slab foundation, drawings also include crawl space foundation

Special features

- 1,240 total square feet of living area
- Kitchen/breakfast area combine for added spaciousness
- Sloped ceiling adds appeal in the sitting area
- The utilities are located on the first floor near the garage
- 2 bedrooms, 1 bath, 2-car garage
- Basement foundation

Second Floor
1,240 sq. ft.

Br 1
11-10x10-7

Kit/Brk
14-10x10-10

R

Dn

P

Br 2
11-9x10-8

L

Sitting
15-0x16-1

Sloped
Ceiling

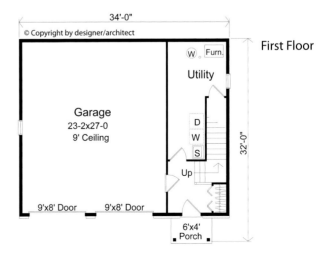

34'-0"

© Copyright by designer/architect

First Floor

W   Furn.

Utility

Garage
23-2x27-0
9' Ceiling

D

W

S

32'-0"

Up

9'x8' Door   9'x8' Door

6'x4'
Porch

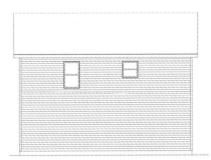

Rear Elevation

Second Floor
691 sq. ft.

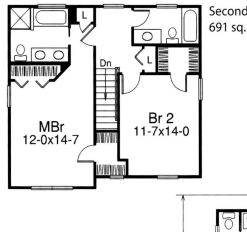

MBr
12-0x14-7

Br 2
11-7x14-0

Dn

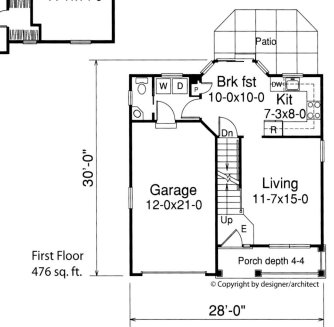

Patio

Brk fst
10-0x10-0

Kit
7-3x8-0

W D P

DW

R

Dn

Garage
12-0x21-0

Living
11-7x15-0

Up

E

30'-0"

First Floor
476 sq. ft.

Porch depth 4-4

© Copyright by designer/architect

28'-0"

Rear Elevation

Special features

- 717 total square feet of living area
- Incline ladder leads up to cozy loft area
- Living room features plenty of windows and a vaulted ceiling
- U-shaped kitchen includes a small bay window at the sink
- 1 bedroom, 1 bath
- Slab foundation

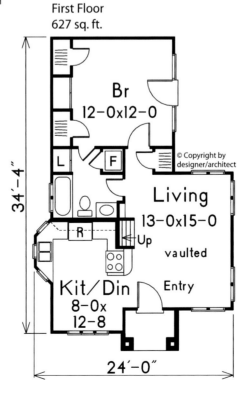

First Floor
627 sq. ft.

Br
12-0x12-0

© Copyright by
designer/architect

Living
13-0x15-0

vaulted

Entry

Kit/Din
8-0x
12-8

34'-4"

24'-0"

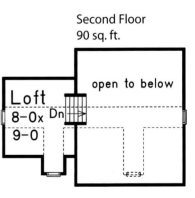

Second Floor
90 sq. ft.

Loft
8-0x
9-0

open to below

Dn

Rear Elevation

Special features

- 864 total square feet of living area
- L-shaped kitchen with convenient pantry is adjacent to dining area
- Easy access to laundry area, linen closet and storage closet
- Both bedrooms include ample closet space
- 2 bedrooms, 1 bath
- Crawl space foundation, drawings also include basement and slab foundations

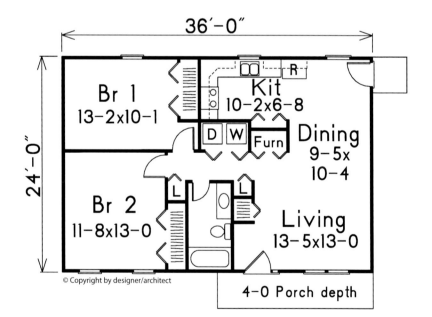

36'-0"

24'-0"

Br 1
13-2x10-1

Kit
10-2x6-8

D W Furn

Dining
9-5x
10-4

Br 2
11-8x13-0

Living
13-5x13-0

4-0 Porch depth

Rear Elevation

Special features

- 2,167 total square feet of living area
- Multi-gables with window shutters and plant boxes combined with stone veneer, create an elegant country facade
- L-shaped kitchen has work island snack bar open to bayed breakfast room and large family room to provide a 40' vista
- Entry and breakfast room access second floor via T-stair
- 4 bedrooms, 2 1/2 baths, 2-car garage
- Basement foundation

Rear Elevation

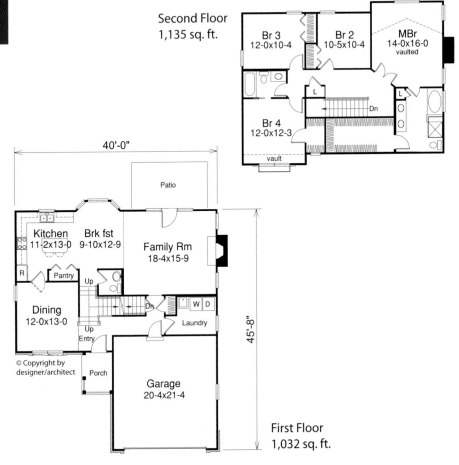

Second Floor
1,135 sq. ft.

Br 3
12-0x10-4

Br 2
10-5x10-4

MBr
14-0x16-0
vaulted

Br 4
12-0x12-3

vault

40'-0"

Patio

Kitchen
11-2x13-0

Brk fst
9-10x12-9

Family Rm
18-4x15-9

Pantry

Up

Dining
12-0x13-0

Dn

W D

Laundry

Up
Entry

45'-8"

© Copyright by
designer/architect

Porch

Garage
20-4x21-4

First Floor
1,032 sq. ft.

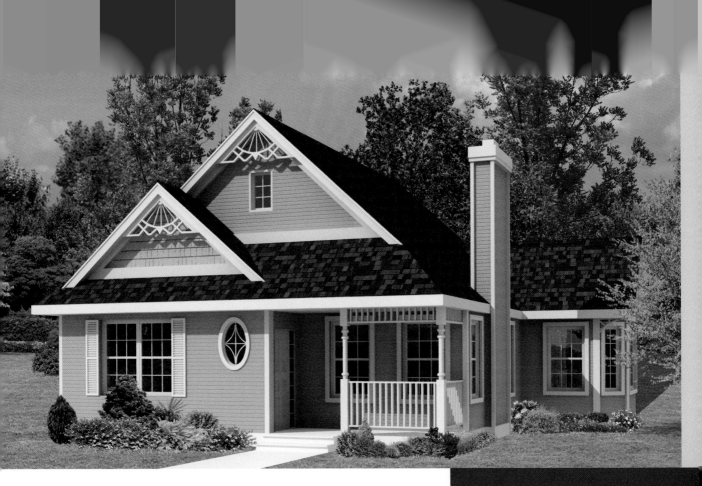

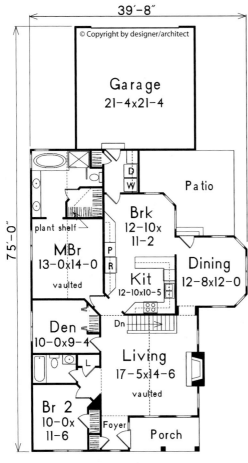

39'-8"

© Copyright by designer/architect

75'-0"

Garage
21-4x21-4

Patio

Brk
12-10x
11-2

D
W

plant shelf →

MBr
13-0x14-0
vaulted

P
R

Kit
12-10x10-5

Dining
12-8x12-0

Den
10-0x9-4

Dn

L

Living
17-5x14-6
vaulted

Br 2
10-0x
11-6

Foyer

Porch

Rear Elevation

Special features

- 1,898 total square feet of living area
- Energy efficient home with 2" x 6" exterior walls
- The great room features a corner fireplace and French doors for outdoor access
- The island kitchen is open to the living areas and has a built-in eating bar and lots of cabinet and counter space
- A second floor loft area overlooks the great room and can serve as a play area
- 3 bedrooms, 2 1/2 baths
- Crawl space foundation

First Floor
1,200 sq. ft.

Second Floor
698 sq. ft.

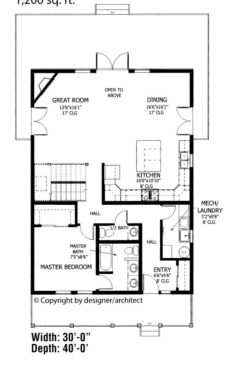

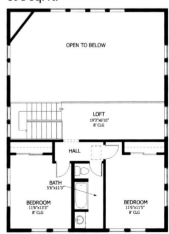

Width: 30'-0"
Depth: 40'-0'

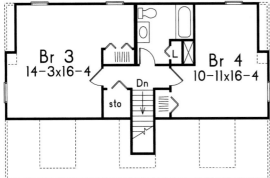

Second Floor
665 sq. ft.

Br 3
14-3x16-4

Br 4
10-11x16-4

Dn

sto

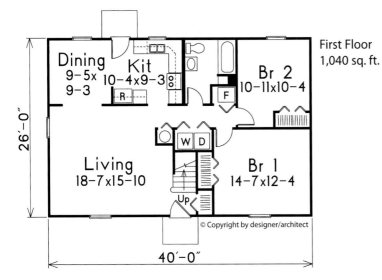

First Floor
1,040 sq. ft.

Dining
9-5x
9-3

Kit
10-4x9-3

R

Br 2
10-11x10-4

F

W D

Living
18-7x15-10

Br 1
14-7x12-4

Up

26'-0"

40'-0"

© Copyright by designer/architect

Special features

- 1,705 total square feet of living area
- Two bedrooms on the first floor for convenience and two bedrooms on the second for privacy
- L-shaped kitchen adjacent to dining room accesses the outdoors
- 2" x 6" exterior walls available, please order plan #598-001D-0110
- 4 bedrooms, 2 baths
- Crawl space foundation, drawings also include basement and slab foundations

Rear Elevation

Special features

- 990 total square feet of living area
- Covered front porch adds a charming feel
- Vaulted ceilings in the kitchen, family and dining rooms create a spacious feel
- Large linen, pantry and storage closets throughout
- 2 bedrooms, 1 bath
- Crawl space foundation

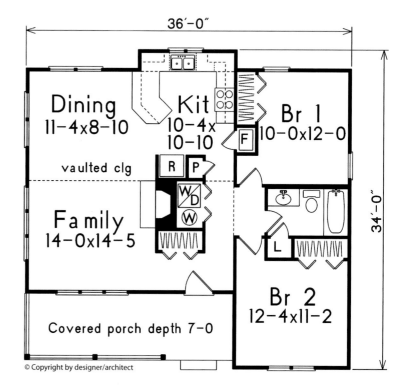

36'-0"

34'-0"

Dining
11-4x8-10

Kit
10-4x
10-10

Br 1
10-0x12-0

vaulted clg

R P

F

W/D

W

L

Family
14-0x14-5

Br 2
12-4x11-2

Covered porch depth 7-0

© Copyright by designer/architect

Rear Elevation

First Floor
1,018 sq. ft.

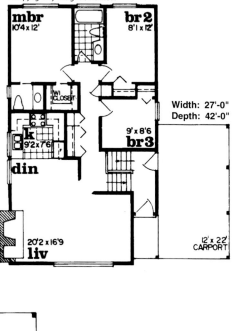

mbr
10'4 x 12'

br 2
8'1 x 12'

k
9'2 x 7'6

9' x 8'6
br3

din

Width: 27'-0"
Depth: 42'-0"

liv
20'2 x 16'9

12' x 22'
CARPORT

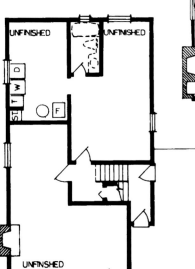

UNFINISHED

UNFINISHED

UNFINISHED

Optional
Lower Level

Special features

- 1,018 total square feet of living area
- Living room enjoys a grand fireplace and a large picture window
- U-shaped compact kitchen offers efficiency
- A half bath is situated in the master bedroom for convenience
- The optional lower level has an additional 1,018 square feet of living area
- 3 bedrooms, 1 1/2 baths, 1-car carport
- Basement foundation

Special features

- 2,066 total square feet of living area
- Large master bedroom includes a sitting area and private bath
- Open living room features a fireplace with built-in bookshelves
- Spacious kitchen accesses formal dining area and breakfast room
- 3 bedrooms, 2 1/2 baths, optional 2-car side entry garage
- Slab foundation

Rear Elevation

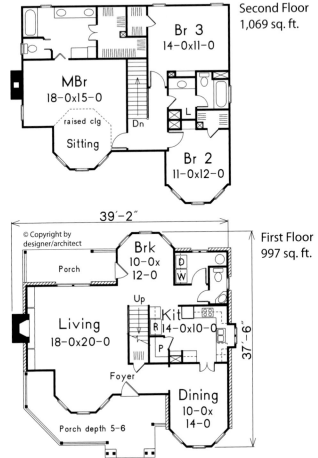

Second Floor
1,069 sq. ft.

Br 3
14-0x11-0

MBr
18-0x15-0

raised clg

Sitting

Dn

L

Br 2
11-0x12-0

39'-2"

© Copyright by
designer/architect

First Floor
997 sq. ft.

Porch

Brk
10-0x
12-0

D
W

Up

Living
18-0x20-0

Kit
14-0x10-0

R

P

37'-6"

Foyer

Dining
10-0x
14-0

Porch depth 5-6

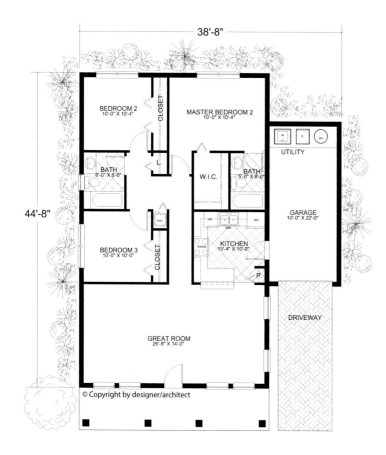

BEDROOM 2
10'-0" X 10'-4"

MASTER BEDROOM 2
10'-0" X 10'-4"

CLOSET

38'-8"

BATH
6'-0" X 8'-0"

W.I.C.

BATH
5'-0" X 8'-0"

UTILITY

W D WH

44'-8"

BEDROOM 3
10'-0" X 10'-0"

CLOSET

KITCHEN
10'-4" X 10'-0"

DW REF

SINK

RANGE

GARAGE
10'-0" X 22'-0"

P.

DRIVEWAY

GREAT ROOM
26'-8" X 14'-0"

Special features

- 1,250 total square feet of living area
- Columns line the covered front porch and usher guests inside
- Only concrete block construction available
- This unique design has an enormous great room creating a spacious gathering area
- 3 bedrooms, 2 baths, 1-car garage
- Slab foundation

Special features

- 2,158 total square feet of living area
- Vaulted entry has a closet and built-in shelves with plant shelf above
- The two-story living room has tall dramatic windows flanking the fireplace and a full-length second floor balcony
- A laundry and half bath are located near the kitchen which has over 30' of counterspace
- 3 bedrooms, 2 1/2 baths, 2-car garage
- Basement foundation

Rear Elevation

30'-0"

58'-0"

Patio

Dining
16-0x12-6

Brk fst
13-0x12-6

Kit
13-0x13-9

Living
16-0x18-11

R

P

W

D

Up

Dn

Entry

Porch

Garage
19-4x21-4

© Copyright by designer/architect

First Floor
1,125 sq. ft.

Br 3
12-7x13-0

Br 2
12-0x12-1

L

Hall

Living Room
Below

Dn

seat

vaulted

MBr
13-0x16-4
vaulted

L

Second Floor
1,033 sq. ft.

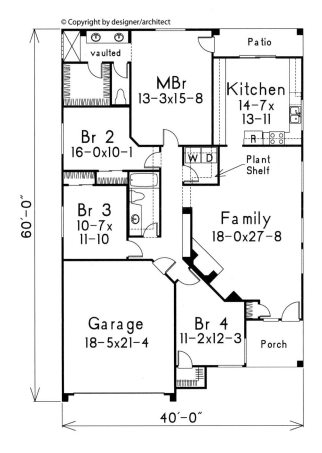

© Copyright by designer/architect

vaulted

MBr
13-3x15-8

Kitchen
14-7 x
13-11

Br 2
16-0x10-1

W D

Plant Shelf

R

Br 3
10-7 x
11-10

Family
18-0x27-8

Patio

60'-0"

Garage
18-5x21-4

Br 4
11-2x12-3

Porch

40'-0"

Special features

■ 1,747 total square feet of living area
■ Entry opens into large family room with coat closet, angled fireplace and attractive plant shelf
■ Kitchen and master bedroom access covered patio
■ Functional kitchen includes ample workspace
■ 4 bedrooms, 2 baths, 2-car garage
■ Slab foundation

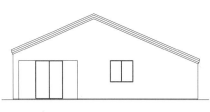

Rear Elevation

Special features

- 2,270 total square feet of living area
- Energy efficient home with 2" x 6" exterior walls
- The galley kitchen has tons of workspace and separates the great room and the vaulted dining room
- The staircase leading to the second floor opens to an elegant loft space overlooking the dining area below
- The master bedroom enjoys its own private covered deck and a bath with separate shower, whirlpool tub and twin sinks
- 4 bedrooms, 2 1/2 baths, 3-car garage
- Crawl space foundation

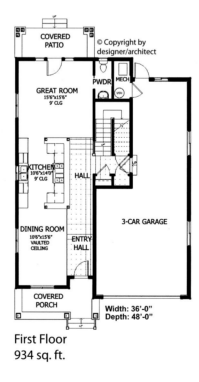

First Floor
934 sq. ft.

Second Floor
1,336 sq. ft.

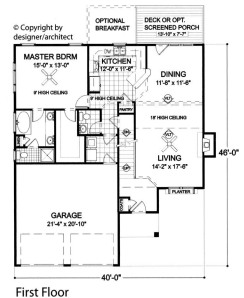

© Copyright by designer/architect

OPTIONAL BREAKFAST

DECK OR OPT. SCREENED PORCH
13'-10" x 7'-7"

MASTER BDRM
15'-0" x 13'-0"

9' HIGH CEILING

KITCHEN
12'-0" x 11'-6"

9' HIGH CEILING

PANTRY

DINING
11'-8" x 11'-6"

18' HIGH CEILING

DN.

18' HIGH CEILING

LIVING
14'-2" x 17'-6"

UP.

PLANTER

COATS

GARAGE
21'-4" x 20'-10"

46'-0"

40'-0"

First Floor
1,131 sq. ft.

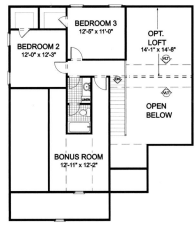

BEDROOM 3
12'-5" x 11'-0"

OPT. LOFT
14'-1" x 14'-8"

BEDROOM 2
12'-0" x 12'-3"

LINEN

DN.

OPEN BELOW

BONUS ROOM
12'-11" x 12'-2"

Second Floor
490 sq. ft.

Special features

- 1,621 total square feet of living area
- 18' ceilings in the living and dining areas add spaciousness
- All bedrooms feature walk-in closets
- Bonus room on the second floor has an additional 257 square feet of living area
- 3 bedrooms, 2 1/2 baths, 2-car garage
- Basement or crawl space foundation, please specify when ordering

Special features

- 1,657 total square feet of living area
- Stylish pass-through between living and dining areas
- Master bedroom is secluded from the living area for privacy
- Large windows in the breakfast and dining areas create a bright and cheerful atmosphere
- 3 bedrooms, 2 1/2 baths, 2-car drive under garage
- Basement foundation

Rear Elevation

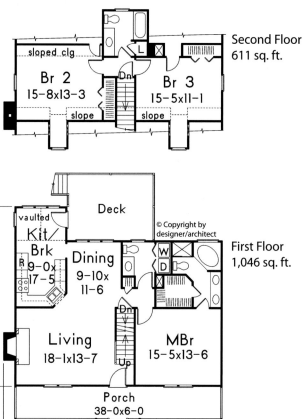

Second Floor
611 sq. ft.

sloped clg

Br 2
15-8x13-3

Dn

Br 3
15-5x11-1

slope   slope

Deck

vaulted

© Copyright by
designer/architect

First Floor
1,046 sq. ft.

Kit/
Brk
9-0x
17-5

Dining
9-10x
11-6

W
D

Dn

Living
18-1x13-7

Up

MBr
15-5x13-6

32'-0"

Porch
38-0x6-0

40'-0"

Special features

- 1,316 total square feet of living area
- Porches are accessible from entry, dining room and bedroom #2
- The living room enjoys a vaulted ceiling, corner fireplace and twin windows with an arched transom
- A kitchen is provided with corner windows, an outdoor plant shelf, a snack bar, a built-in pantry and opens to a large dining room
- Bedrooms feature walk-in closets and have access to oversized baths
- 2 bedrooms, 2 baths, 2-car side entry garage
- Basement foundation, drawings also include crawl space and slab foundations

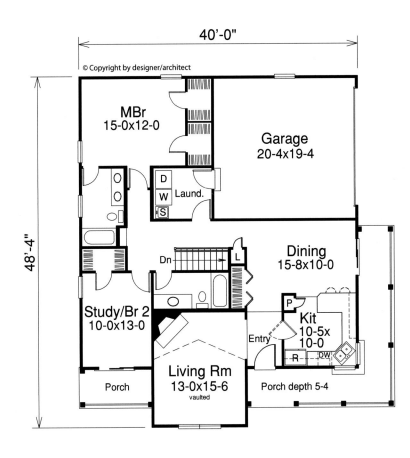

40'-0"

© Copyright by designer/architect

MBr
15-0x12-0

Garage
20-4x19-4

D
W   Laund.
S

Dn

Dining
15-8x10-0

48'-4"

Study/Br 2
10-0x13-0

L

Entry

P

Kit
10-5x
10-0

R   DW

Porch

Living Rm
13-0x15-6
vaulted

Porch depth 5-4

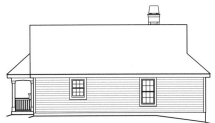

Rear Elevation

Special features

- 1,112 total square feet of living area
- Energy efficient home with 2" x 6" exterior walls
- Brick, an arched window and planter box decorate the facade of this lovely ranch home
- The eat-in kitchen offers an abundance of counterspace and enjoys access to the outdoors
- Three bedrooms are situated together for easy family living
- 3 bedrooms, 1 bath
- Basement foundation

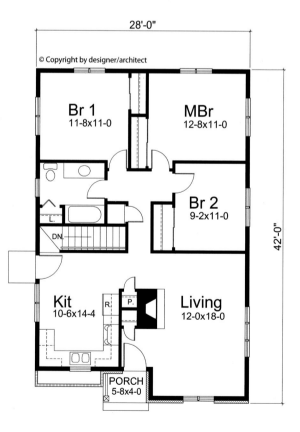

28'-0"

© Copyright by designer/architect

Br 1
11-8x11-0

MBr
12-8x11-0

Br 2
9-2x11-0

DN.

L.

R.

P.

Kit
10-6x14-4

Living
12-0x18-0

42'-0"

PORCH
5-8x4-0

© Copyright by designer/architect

MASTER BEDROOM
13-2 x 14-2

MST BATH

BATH

BEDROOM
10-7 x 12-0

WALK-IN CLOSET

WH

FURNACE

LAUNDRY

BEDROOM
10-7 x 10-0

DECK

DINING
13-0 x 10-1

GREAT ROOM
17-8 x 12-0

KITCHEN
13-0 x 11-6

DW

COVERED PORCH
20-0 x 12-0

Width: 36'-0"
Depth: 50'-0"

Special features

- 1,388 total square feet of living area
- Energy efficient home with 2" x 6" exterior walls
- A stone-lined covered porch adds a superb outdoor living area and decorates the exterior
- The efficient kitchen offers a counter that opens to the dining room and enjoys the great room nearby
- A lovely master bedroom retreat is equipped with a private bath, walk-in closet and sliding glass doors leading to the rear yard
- 3 bedrooms, 2 baths
- Crawl space foundation

Special features

- 1,539 total square feet of living area
- This two-story home is ideal for a narrow lot
- The front half of the first floor consists of the combined family room, kitchen and dining area while the rear houses the master bedroom, utility and half bath
- Two secondary bedrooms and a bath on the second floor round out this efficient design
- 3 bedrooms, 2 1/2 baths, 2-car rear entry garage
- Slab foundation

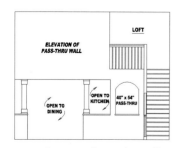

Elevation of Pass-Through Wall

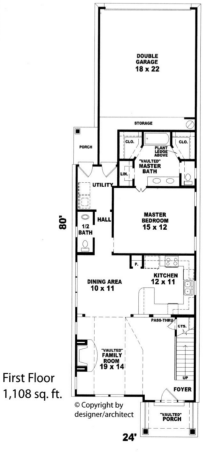

First Floor
1,108 sq. ft.

© Copyright by designer/architect

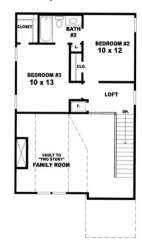

Second Floor
431 sq. ft.

Special features

- 1,647 total square feet of living area
- Enormous great room boasts a vaulted ceiling
- Located in the great room is an open kitchen with an island and breakfast bar
- Stunning loft overlooks the great room
- 2 bedrooms, 1 bath
- Slab or basement foundation, please specify when ordering

First Floor
1,288 sq. ft.

BEDROOM 1
11'-10" x 10'-0"

BEDROOM 2
11'-4" x 10'-0"

COATS

46'-0"
+ PORCH

LINEN

PANTRY

© Copyright by
designer/architect

GREAT ROOM
27'-4" x 29'-5"
20' HIGH CEILING

VAULT   VAULT

DECK/PATIO
11'-6" x 18'-8"

DECK
7'-6" x 36'-0"

PORCH
24'-4" x 7'-6"

28'-0"
+ DECKS/PATIO

Second Floor
359 sq. ft.

VAULT   VAULT

LOFT
23'-1" x 15'-6"

40" KNEE WALL

DN

OPEN BELOW
20' HIGH CEILING

VAULT   VAULT

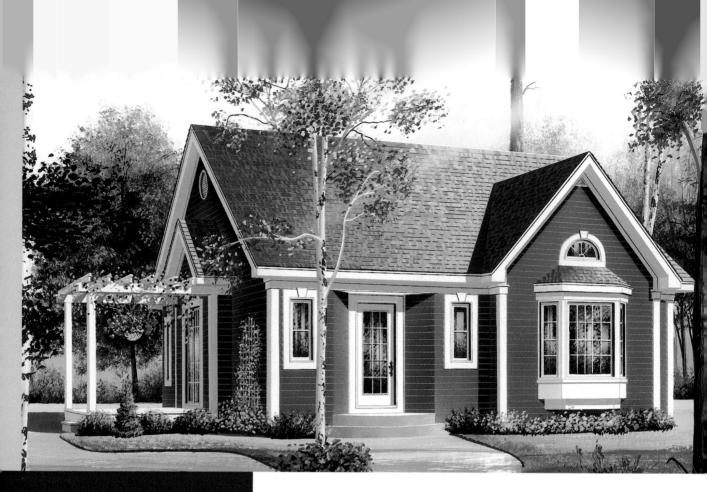

Special features

- 1,199 total square feet of living area
- Energy efficient home with 2" x 6" exterior walls
- Open living spaces are ideal for entertaining
- Spacious kitchen has lots of extra counterspace
- Nice-sized bedrooms are separated by a full bath
- 2 bedrooms, 1 bath
- Basement foundation

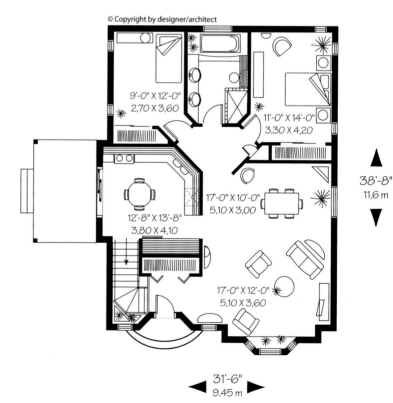

© Copyright by designer/architect

9'-0" X 12'-0"
2,70 X 3,60

11'-0" X 14'-0"
3,30 X 4,20

12'-8" X 13'-8"
3,80 X 4,10

17'-0" X 10'-0"
5,10 X 3,00

17'-0" X 12'-0"
5,10 X 3,60

38'-8"
11,6 m

31'-6"
9,45 m

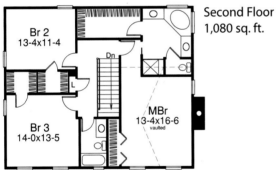

Second Floor
1,080 sq. ft.

Br 2
13-4x11-4

Dn

MBr
13-4x16-6
vaulted

Br 3
14-0x13-5

36'-0"

© Copyright by designer/architect

Patio

First Floor
970 sq. ft.

30'-0"

Brk fst

W Laun.
D
Screened Porch
13-4x9-0

Kit
14-0x18-0

Dn

P
L

Living
13-2x20-0

Up

Dining
13-1x11-0
tray

Entry

Porch depth 6-4

Special features

- 2,050 total square feet of living area
- Large living room with fireplace enjoys a view to front porch and access to rear screened porch
- L-shaped kitchen has a built-in pantry, island snack bar and breakfast area with bay window
- Master bedroom is vaulted with a luxury bath and ample closet space
- 3 bedrooms, 2 1/2 baths, 2-car detached garage
- Basement foundation, drawings also include slab and crawl space foundations

Rear Elevation

Special features

- 1,260 total square feet of living area
- A bayed breakfast room is an extension of the compact kitchen
- Convenient first floor master bedroom includes a full bath
- Two secondary bedrooms share a full bath
- 3 bedrooms, 2 baths
- Basement foundation

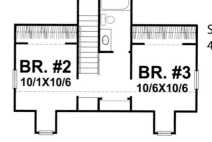

BR. #2
10/1X10/6

BR. #3
10/6X10/6

Second Floor
450 sq. ft.

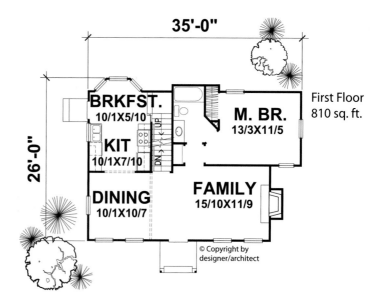

35'-0"

26'-0"

BRKFST.
10/1X5/10

KIT
10/1X7/10

DINING
10/1X10/7

M. BR.
13/3X11/5

FAMILY
15/10X11/9

First Floor
810 sq. ft.

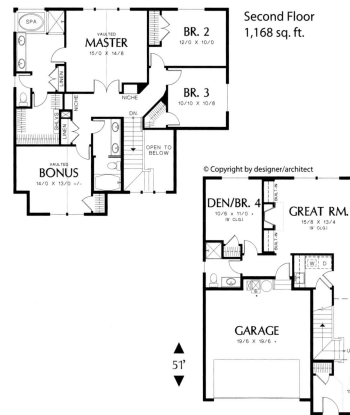

Second Floor
1,168 sq. ft.

SPA

VAULTED
MASTER
15/0 X 14/8

BR. 2
12/0 X 10/0

BR. 3
10/10 X 10/8

NICHE

LINEN

LINEN

NICHE

SHLVS.

DN.

OPEN TO BELOW

VAULTED
BONUS
14/0 X 13/0 +/-

First Floor
1,252 sq. ft.

© Copyright by designer/architect

DEN/BR. 4
10/6 x 11/0 +
(9' CLG.)

GREAT RM.
15/8 X 13/4
(9' CLG.)

NOOK
8/6 X 9/4 +/-
(9' CLG.)

DESK

BUILT-IN

BUILT-IN

W   D

11/8 X 11/10 +/-
(9' CLG.)

PAN   REF

GARAGE
19/6 X 19/6 +

UP

51'

VAULTED
LIV/DIN
15/2 X 20/6 +/-

40'

PORCH

Special features

- 2,420 total square feet of living area
- Energy efficient home with 2" x 6" exterior walls
- A grand master suite has a double-door entry, spacious bath with spa tub and a large walk-in closet
- Den/bedroom #4 has easy access to a full bath and is secluded from other bedrooms
- Central living areas combine for maximum living space
- Second floor bonus room is included in the square footage
- 3 bedrooms, 3 baths, 2-car garage
- Crawl space foundation

Special features

- 1,020 total square feet of living area
- Kitchen features open stairs, pass-through to great room, pantry and deck access
- Master bedroom features private entrance to bath, large walk-in closet and sliding doors to deck
- Informal entrance into home through the garage
- Great room has a vaulted ceiling and fireplace
- 2 bedrooms, 1 bath, 2-car garage
- Basement foundation

Rear Elevation

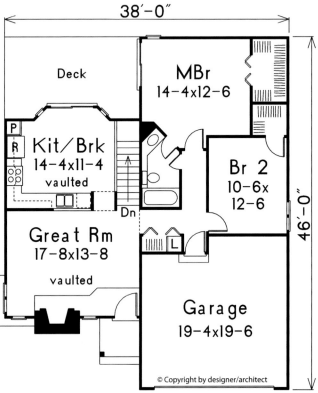

38'-0"

46'-0"

Deck

MBr
14-4x12-6

Kit/Brk
14-4x11-4
vaulted

P
R

Dn

Br 2
10-6x
12-6

Great Rm
17-8x13-8

vaulted

L

Garage
19-4x19-6

© Copyright by designer/architect

- 2,046 total square feet of living area
- Hipped roof and special brickwork provide nice curb appeal
- The kitchen and breakfast room offer island cabinetry, a walk-in pantry, a wide bay window and easy access to a large dining room
- Cheery transom windows and fireplace are just two amenities of the huge great room
- 4 bedrooms, 2 1/2 baths, 2-car garage
- Basement foundation

First Floor
1,031 sq. ft.

37'-0"

Patio

Brk fst.
10-6x14-1

Kitchen
10-6x12-1

Great Room
13-4x21-6

Dn

R

P

Dining
17-4x11-0
tray clg.

D W S

Up

Entry

49-8"

Porch depth 5-4

© Copyright by
designer/architect

Garage
19-4x20-4

Second Floor
1,015 sq. ft.

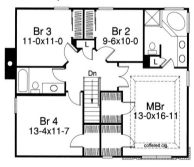

Br 3
11-0x11-0

Br 2
9-6x10-0

L

L

Dn

Br 4
13-4x11-7

MBr
13-0x16-11

coffered clg.

Rear Elevation

Special features

- 1,978 total square feet of living area
- Energy efficient home with 2" x 6" exterior walls
- Designed for a sloping lot, this multi-level home intrigues the eye
- Sunlight filters into the grand two-story foyer and living room from tall windows
- Master suite has elegant front-facing windows and a private bath
- 3 bedrooms, 2 1/2 baths, 2-car drive under garage
- Basement foundation

BR. 3
11/0 X 10/8

BR. 2
11/0 X 10/0

DN

LOFT

FOYER
BELOW

©Alan Mascord Design Associates, Inc.

LIN

LIVING
BELOW

VAULTED
MASTER
15/2 X 12/0

Second Floor
872 sq. ft.

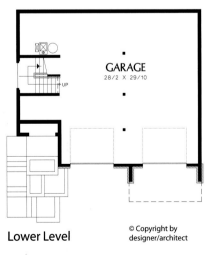

GARAGE
28/2 X 29/10

UP

Lower Level

© Copyright by
designer/architect

OPT FR
DRS.

DW
15/0 X 9/0

PAN

DINING
10/6 X 12/0+

DN

NOOK
13/10 X 8/4

UP

DN

2 STORY
LIVING
13/0 X 14/0

FAMILY
13/10 X 20/8

▲
35'
▼

DECK

◀ 38' ▶

First Floor
1,106 sq. ft.

Lower Level
976 sq. ft.

COVERED
PATIO

BEDROOM
11'8"x10'7"
8' CLG

BATH

REC ROOM
17'2"x17'0"
8' CLG

BEDROOM
11'8"x10'7"
8' CLG

UTILITY
9'4"x7'11"

F.AU

MECH

GARAGE

First Floor
1,384 sq. ft.

Width: 32'-0"
Depth: 56'-0"

COVERED
DECK

MASTER
BEDROOM
14'0"x14'10"
9' CLG

GREAT ROOM
14'8"x19'6"
9' CLG

MASTER
CLOSET

MSTR
BATH

PWDR

KITCHEN
9'4"x13'0"
9' CLG

DINING
ROOM
11'8"x12'0"
9' CLG

LIVING ROOM
15'0"x12'0"
9' CLG

© Copyright by
designer/architect

Special features

- 2,360 total square feet of living area
- Energy efficient home with 2" x 6" exterior walls
- Step up to the first floor to view the stunning open living space with the central kitchen as a focal point and natural gathering spot
- The living room enjoys French doors leading to a front balcony while the great room features access to the rear covered deck
- A recreation room on the lower level offers ample room for casual parties and includes access to a covered patio
- 3 bedrooms, 2 1/2 baths, 2-car garage
- Crawl space foundation

Special features

- 2,054 total square feet of living area
- A sweeping porch leads to the large foyer with staircase, powder room and handy coat closet
- Spacious living room has a fireplace and triple doors to the patio
- Kitchen features an island counter and breakfast area with bay window
- Large master bedroom has two spacious closets and accesses a luxury bath
- 3 bedrooms, 2 1/2 baths, 2-car detached garage
- Basement foundation

Rear Elevation

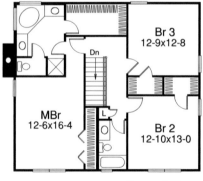

Second Floor
1,020 sq. ft.

Br 3
12-9x12-8

MBr
12-6x16-4

Br 2
12-10x13-0

Dn

First Floor
1,034 sq. ft.

34'-0"

Patio

© Copyright by designer/architect

Brk fst

Living
12-6x20-0

Dn

W
D
L

Kit
13-0x18-0

Up

Dining
12-8x10-8

Computer
11-0x9-0

30'-0"

R

Porch depth 6-4

Second Floor
570 sq. ft.

STORAGE   STORAGE

Br 2
14-4x11-6

Br 3
15-6x11-6

STORAGE

36'-0"

Study
9-5x10-8

Kit
9-8x13-0

DN.

UP

R.

First Floor
1,104 sq. ft.

38'-4"

Dining
8-0x9-2

MBr
13-8x11-4

Living
12-4x19-8

© Copyright by
designer/architect

Special features

- 1,674 total square feet of living area
- Energy efficient home with 2" x 6" exterior walls
- Covered entrance opens to find open living and dining rooms that are designed for entertaining
- A quiet study could also be used as a guest bedroom
- The master bedroom is secluded on the first floor while two additional bedrooms share the second floor
- 3 bedrooms, 2 baths
- Basement foundation

Special features

- 864 total square feet of living area
- Charming front porch welcomes guests and provides a wonderful place to relax
- The expansive living/dining room shares a snack bar with the kitchen
- The kitchen provides an abundance of storage with a nice pantry and cabinets
- Two generously sized bedrooms share a full bath and are separated from the main living areas for privacy
- 2 bedrooms, 1 bath
- Slab or crawl space foundation, please specify when ordering

LAUNDRY
12'-0"X6'-0"

KITCHEN
11'-10"x9'-10"

snack bar

BEDROOM 2
13'-0" x 10'-0"

BEDROOM 1
13'-0" x 10'-0"

LIVING/DINING ROOM
20'-0"x14'-0"

36'-0"

6' WIDE COVERED PORCH

33'-0"

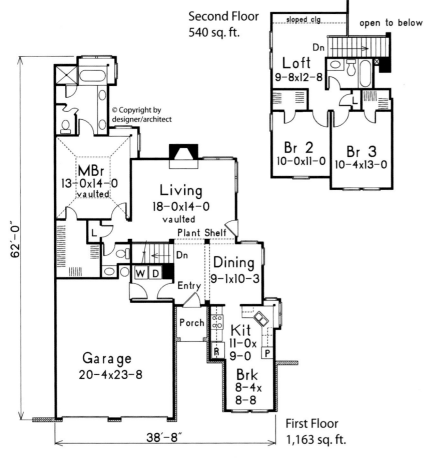

Second Floor
540 sq. ft.

sloped clg

open to below

Dn

Loft
9-8x12-8

Br 2
10-0x11-0

Br 3
10-4x13-0

© Copyright by
designer/architect

MBr
13-0x14-0
vaulted

Living
18-0x14-0
vaulted

Plant Shelf

Dn

Dining
9-1x10-3

W D

Entry

Porch

Kit
11-0x
9-0

R

P

Brk
8-4x
8-8

Garage
20-4x23-8

62'-0"

38'-8"

First Floor
1,163 sq. ft.

Rear Elevation

Special features

- 1,498 total square feet of living area
- A perfect home for a narrow and sloping lot featuring both front and rear garages
- Large living room has fireplace, rear outdoor balcony and a pass-through snack bar to a spacious U-shaped kitchen with adjacent dining area
- Roomy master bedroom with luxury bath and two walk-in closets
- 2 bedrooms, 2 1/2 baths, 1-car garage and a 2-car rear entry drive-under garage
- Walk-out basement foundation

Rear Elevation

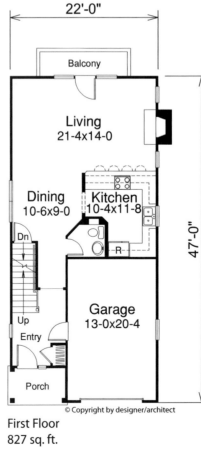

22'-0"

Balcony

Living
21-4x14-0

47'-0"

Dining
10-6x9-0

Kitchen
10-4x11-8

Dn

R

Up

Entry

Garage
13-0x20-4

Porch

© Copyright by designer/architect

First Floor
827 sq. ft.

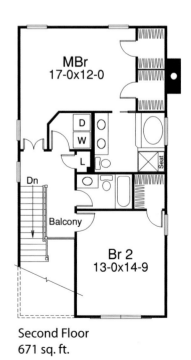

MBr
17-0x12-0

D

W

L

Dn

Balcony

Br 2
13-0x14-9

Seat

Second Floor
671 sq. ft.

BR. 2
12/0 X 10/0
(9' CLG.)

BR. 3
12/0 X 10/8
(9' CLG.)

LOFT
14/2 X 7/0
(9' CLG.)

DN.

GREAT RM
BELOW

VAULTED
MASTER
14/0 X 16/0

Second Floor
960 sq. ft.

Special features

- 2,262 total square feet of living area
- Energy efficient home with 2" x 6" exterior walls
- All bedrooms are located on the second floor for privacy
- Formal dining room is cheerful and sunny with two walls of windows
- Great room has access to a deck
- 3 bedrooms, 2 1/2 baths, 2-car drive under garage
- Basement foundation

SHOP
8/10 X 8/4

GARAGE
29/8 X 31/10

UP

STORAGE

Lower Level

© Copyright by designer/architect

NOOK
9/0 X 10/8 +/-
(9' CLG.)

DINING
11/0 X 16/0
(9' CLG.)

12/6 X 12/6 +/-

REF.

DN.

UP

DN.

PAN.

MEDIA
CENTER

2 STORY
GREAT RM.
15/6 X 16/0

DEN
12/2 X 12/0
(9' CLG.)

BUILT-IN

DECK

PLANTER

40'

First Floor
1,302 sq. ft. ◄ 40' ►

Special features

- 1,200 total square feet of living area
- Enjoy lazy summer evenings on this magnificent porch
- Activity area has a fireplace and ascending stair to the cozy loft
- Kitchen features a built-in pantry
- Master bedroom enjoys a large bath, walk-in closet and cozy loft overlooking the room below
- 2 bedrooms, 2 baths
- Crawl space foundation

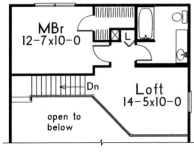

Second Floor
416 sq. ft.

MBr
12-7x10-0

L

Loft
14-5x10-0

Dn

open to below

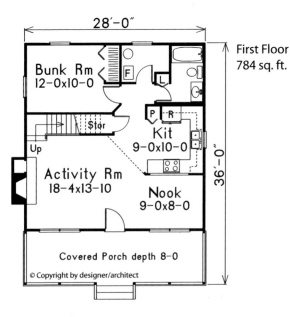

28'-0"

First Floor
784 sq. ft.

Bunk Rm
12-0x10-0

F

L

Stor

Up

P R

Kit
9-0x10-0

Activity Rm
18-4x13-10

Nook
9-0x8-0

36'-0"

Covered Porch depth 8-0

© Copyright by designer/architect

Second Floor
518 sq. ft.

DECK

MBr
12-2x14-10

Br
10-10x11-5

Balcony   DN.

Open to Below

First Floor
760 sq. ft.

SCREENED PORCH
11-3x7-8

Dining
10-9x11-5

Kit
11-3x11-5

Laundry

34'-0"

Great Rm
19-0x13-2

R

DN

PORCH
12-0x6-0

© Copyright by designer/architect

32'-0"

Special features

- 1,203 total square feet of living area
- Large porch for quiet evening relaxation
- The living room features a vaulted ceiling, fireplace and dining area with patio views
- The kitchen includes an abundance of cabinet storage, a large walk-in pantry and door to the rear yard
- The master bedroom has a vaulted ceiling, private bath with built-in linen storage and a walk-in closet
- 4 bedrooms, 2 1/2 baths, 2-car garage
- Basement foundation, drawings also include slab and crawl space foundations

Rear Elevation

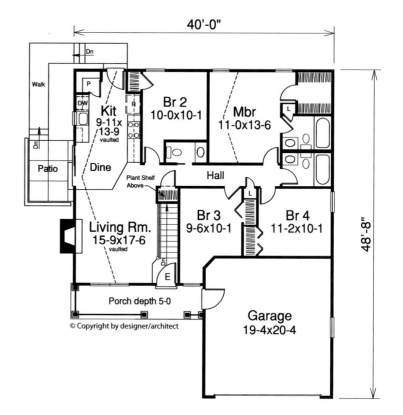

40'-0"

48'-8"

Dn

Walk

P

DW

Dn

Kit
9-11x
13-9
vaulted

Br 2
10-0x10-1

Mbr
11-0x13-6

L

Dine

Patio

Plant Shelf
Above

Hall

L

Living Rm.
15-9x17-6
vaulted

Br 3
9-6x10-1

Br 4
11-2x10-1

E

Porch depth 5-0

Garage
19-4x20-4

© Copyright by designer/architect

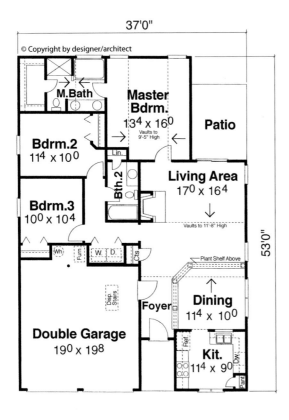

37'0"

© Copyright by designer/architect

M.Bath

Master Bdrm.
13⁴ x 16⁰
Vaults to 9'-5" High

Patio

Bdrm.2
11⁴ x 10⁰

Lin.

Bth.2

Living Area
17⁰ x 16⁴
Vaults to 11'-8" High

Bdrm.3
10⁰ x 10⁴

Wh Furn. W. D. Cts.

Plant Shelf Above

Disp Stairs

Foyer

Dining
11⁴ x 10⁰

Double Garage
19⁰ x 19⁸

Ref.

Kit.
11⁴ x 9⁰

Pant.

Dw.

53'0"

Special features

- 1,365 total square feet of living area
- Plant shelf above the dining area creates interest to the interior
- Direct access from the master bedroom into the living area
- Vaulted living area focuses on a centered fireplace
- 3 bedrooms, 2 baths, 2-car garage
- Basement or slab foundation, please specify when ordering

Special features

- 1,548 total square feet of living area
- Designed perfectly for a narrow lot, this home has plenty of space for family living
- A convenient laundry room connects the garage to the breakfast room
- The cozy den has a double-door entry offering seclusion and making it ideal as a home office
- 2 bedrooms, 2 baths, 2-car side entry garage
- Basement foundation

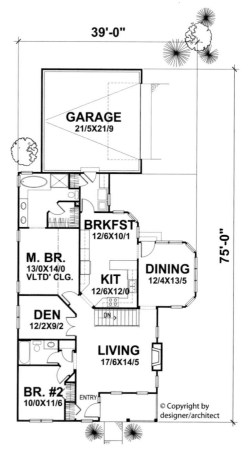

39'-0"

75'-0"

GARAGE
21/5X21/9

BRKFST
12/6X10/1

M. BR.
13/0X14/0
VLTD' CLG.

KIT
12/6X12/0

DINING
12/4X13/5

DEN
12/2X9/2

DN

LIVING
17/6X14/5

BR. #2
10/0X11/6

ENTRY

© Copyright by
designer/architect

Special features

- 1,524 total square feet of living area
- Delightful balcony overlooks two-story entry illuminated by an oval window
- Roomy first floor master bedroom offers quiet privacy
- All bedrooms feature one or more walk-in closets
- 3 bedrooms, 2 1/2 baths, 2-car garage
- Basement foundation, drawings also include crawl space and slab foundations

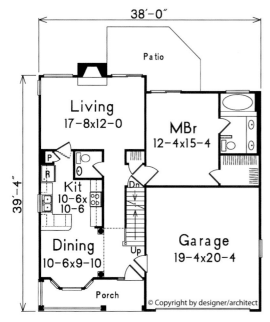

38'-0"

39'-4"

Patio

Living
17-8x12-0

MBr
12-4x15-4

Kit
10-6x 10-6

P
R

Dn

Dining
10-6x9-10

Up

Garage
19-4x20-4

Porch

© Copyright by designer/architect

First Floor
951 sq. ft.

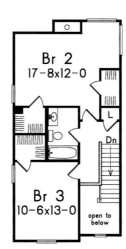

Br 2
17-8x12-0

L

Dn

Br 3
10-6x13-0

open to below

Second Floor
573 sq. ft.

Special features

- 1,260 total square feet of living area
- Living area features an enormous stone fireplace and sliding glass doors for accessing the deck
- Kitchen/dining area is organized with lots of cabinet and counterspace
- Second floor bedroom is vaulted and has closet space along one entire wall
- 3 bedrooms, 1 bath
- Crawl space foundation

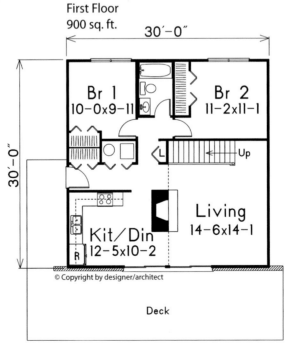

First Floor
900 sq. ft.

30'-0"

30'-0"

Br 1
10-0x9-11

Br 2
11-2x11-1

Up

Kit/Din
12-5x10-2

Living
14-6x14-1

R

L

© Copyright by designer/architect

Deck

Second Floor
360 sq. ft.

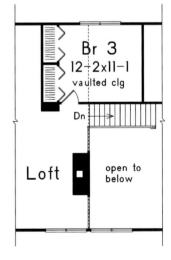

Br 3
12-2x11-1
vaulted clg

Dn

Loft

open to below

Second Floor
604 sq. ft.

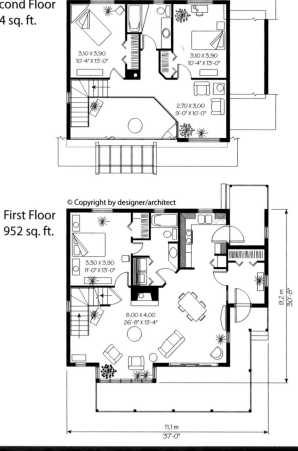

3,10 X 3,90
10'-4" X 13'-0"

3,10 X 3,90
10'-4" X 13'-0"

2,70 X 3,00
9'-0" X 10'-0"

Special features

- 1,556 total square feet of living area
- Energy efficient home with 2" x 6" exterior walls
- Master bedroom has a walk-in closet
- Separate entry with closet is a unique feature
- 3 bedrooms, 2 baths
- Basement foundation

© Copyright by designer/architect

First Floor
952 sq. ft.

3,30 X 3,90
11'-0" X 13'-0"

8,00 X 4,00
26'-8" X 13'-4"

9,2 m
30'-8"

11,1 m
37'-0"

Special features

- 1,339 total square feet of living area
- Full-length covered porch enhances front facade
- Vaulted ceiling and stone fireplace add drama to the family room
- Walk-in closets in the bedrooms provide ample storage space
- Combined kitchen/dining area adjoins the family room for the perfect entertaining space
- 2" x 6" exterior walls available, please order plan #598-058D-0072
- 3 bedrooms, 2 1/2 baths
- Crawl space foundation

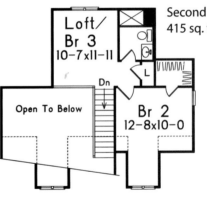

Second Floor
415 sq. ft.

Loft/
Br 3
10-7x11-11

Open To Below

Dn

L

Br 2
12-8x10-0

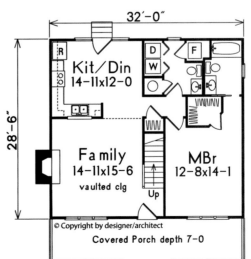

32'-0"

First Floor
924 sq. ft.

Kit/Din
14-11x12-0

28'-6"

Family
14-11x15-6
vaulted clg

MBr
12-8x14-1

Up

© Copyright by designer/architect

Covered Porch depth 7-0

Rear Elevation

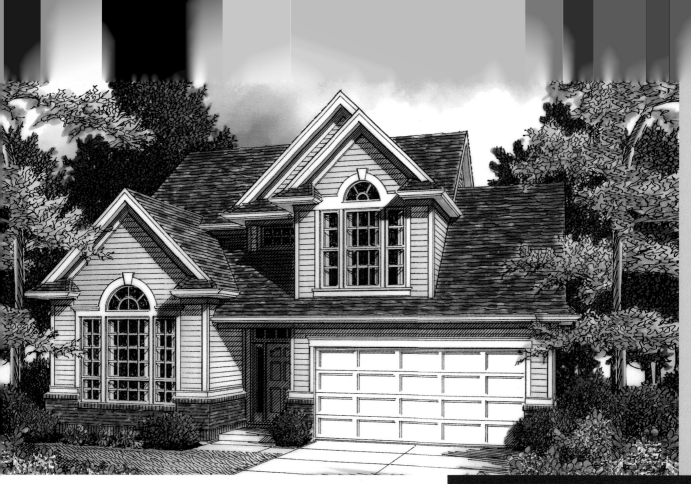

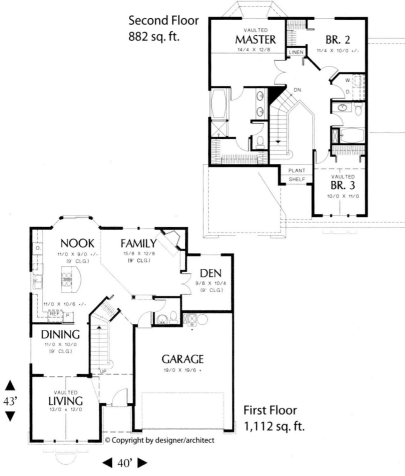

Second Floor
882 sq. ft.

VAULTED
MASTER
14/4 X 12/8

LINEN

BR. 2
11/4 X 10/0 +/-

DN.

W.
D.

PLANT
SHELF

VAULTED
BR. 3
10/0 X 11/0

NOOK
11/0 X 9/0 +/-
(9' CLG.)

FAMILY
15/8 X 12/8
(9' CLG.)

DEN
9/8 X 10/4
(9' CLG.)

11/0 X 10/6 +/-

REF.

DINING
11/0 X 10/0
(9' CLG.)

UP

GARAGE
19/0 X 19/6 +

VAULTED
LIVING
13/0 x 12/0

43'

40'

© Copyright by designer/architect

First Floor
1,112 sq. ft.

Special features

- 1,994 total square feet of living area
- Energy efficient home with 2" x 6" exterior walls
- Breakfast nook overlooks the kitchen and family room creating an airy feeling
- A double-door entry off the family room leads to a cozy den ideal as a home office
- Master suite has a walk-in closet and private bath
- 3 bedrooms, 2 1/2 baths, 2-car garage
- Crawl space foundation

Special features

- 1,116 total square feet of living area
- Centrally located kitchen serves the breakfast and dining areas with ease
- Fireplace warms the vaulted family room which is open and spacious
- Vaulted master bedroom enjoys two closets, a private bath and access to the outdoors
- 3 bedrooms, 2 baths, 1-car garage
- Crawl space or slab foundation, please specify when ordering

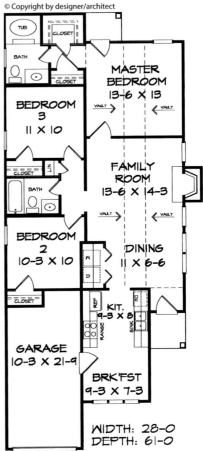

TUB

CLOSET

BATH

CLOSET

MASTER BEDROOM
13-6 X 13

VAULT

VAULT

BEDROOM 3
11 X 10

CLOSET

LIN

FAMILY ROOM
13-6 X 14-3

BATH

VAULT

VAULT

BEDROOM 2
10-3 X 10

DINING
11 X 6-6

W

D

CLOSET

REF

KIT.
9-3 X 8

RANGE

SINK

RG

GARAGE
10-3 X 21-9

BRK'FST
9-3 X 7-3

WIDTH: 28-0
DEPTH: 61-0

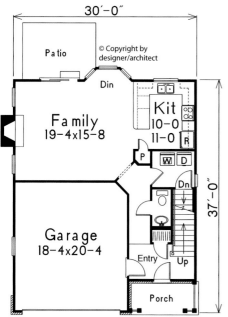

30'-0"

Patio

© Copyright by
designer/architect

Din

Family
19-4x15-8

Kit
10-0
11-0

R

P

W D

Dn

37'-0"

Garage
18-4x20-4

Entry Up

Porch

First Floor
680 sq. ft.

Br 2
13-7x11-3

Br 3
11-0x12-11

Dn

L

MBr
18-4x12-0

plant shelf

Second Floor
991 sq. ft.

Special features

- 1,671 total square feet of living area
- Triple gables and stone facade create great curb appeal
- Two-story entry with hallway leads to the family room, dining area with bay window and U-shaped kitchen
- Second floor features a large master bedroom with luxury bath, overlook to entry and two secondary bedrooms with hall bath
- 3 bedrooms, 2 1/2 baths, 2-car garage
- Basement foundation

Rear Elevation

Special features

- 1,280 total square feet of living area
- A front porch deck, ornate porch roof, massive stone fireplace and Old-English windows all generate an inviting appearance
- The large living room accesses the kitchen and spacious dining area
- Two spacious bedrooms with ample closet space comprise the second floor
- 4 bedrooms, 2 baths
- Basement foundation, drawings also include slab and crawl space foundations

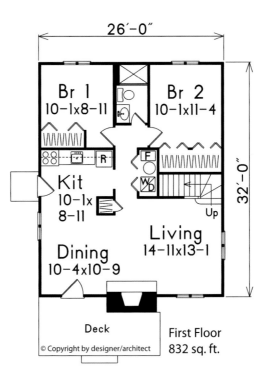

26'-0"

32'-0"

Br 1
10-1x8-11

Br 2
10-1x11-4

Kit
10-1x
8-11

Living
14-11x13-1

Up

Dining
10-4x10-9

Deck

© Copyright by designer/architect

First Floor
832 sq. ft.

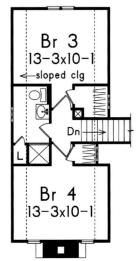

Second Floor
448 sq. ft.

Br 3
13-3x10-1

sloped clg

Dn

L

Br 4
13-3x10-1

Special features

- 1,397 total square feet of living area
- Den with rock hearth fireplace opens to dining area and kitchen
- Kitchen and dining area have an eat-in bar with access to a rear grilling porch
- Second floor bedrooms have unique ceilings and lots of closet space
- 3 bedrooms, 2 baths
- Crawl space or slab foundation, please specify when ordering

31'-8"

38'-4"

KITCHEN
9'-4" X 10'-10"

REF PANTRY
RG
DW

GRILLING PORCH
11'-8" X 6'-0"

DINING
10'-0" X 13'-6"

SUPPLY ROOM

WH

BATH

STACK W/D

DEN
15'-6" X 18'-10"

BEDROOM 1
11'-4" X 11'-0"

UP

COVERED PORCH
20'-0" X 8'-0"

First Floor
890 sq. ft.

BATH

5' WALL

LIN

8' LINE

BEDROOM 3
11'-4" X 12'-8"

BEDROOM 2
13'-4" X 14'-6"

8' LINE

DN

5' WALL

4' WALL

Second Floor
507 sq. ft.

Special features

- 713 total square feet of living area
- An attractive exterior has been created with the use of arches, stonework and a roof dormer
- The living room features a dining area with bay window and a separate entry with access to garage
- L-shaped kitchen has view to the rear yard and a built-in pantry
- The second floor offers a large bedroom with alcove for a desk, walk-in closet and a private bath off the hall
- 1 bedroom, 1 1/2 baths, 2-car garage, RV garage
- Slab foundation

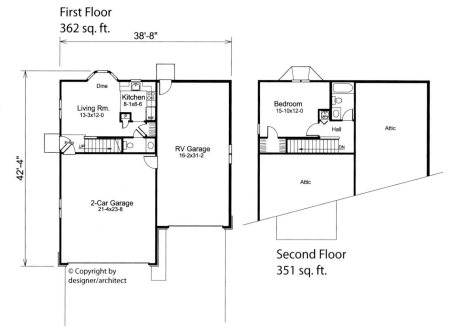

First Floor
362 sq. ft.

38'-8"

42'-4"

Dine

Kitchen
8-1x8-6

Living Rm.
13-3x12-0

Entry

UP

RV Garage
16-2x31-2

2-Car Garage
21-4x23-8

© Copyright by
designer/architect

Bedroom
15-10x12-0

Hall

Attic

Attic

DN

Second Floor
351 sq. ft.

Rear Elevation

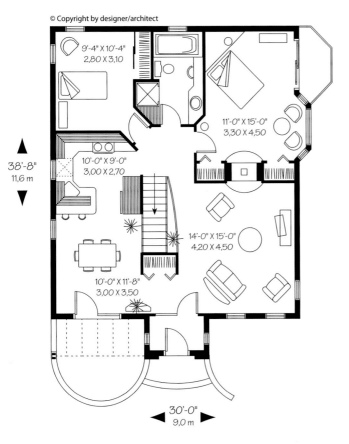

© Copyright by designer/architect

9'-4" X 10'-4"
2,80 X 3,10

11'-0" X 15'-0"
3,30 X 4,50

10'-0" X 9'-0"
3,00 X 2,70

14'-0" X 15'-0"
4,20 X 4,50

10'-0" X 11'-8"
3,00 X 3,50

38'-8"
11,6 m

30'-0"
9,0 m

Special features

- 1,066 total square feet of living area
- Energy efficient home with 2" x 6" exterior walls
- Separate front hall with closet makes an interesting entrance
- Family room has see-through fireplace which it shares with the master bedroom
- Dining area has access to an outdoor balcony/patio
- 2 bedrooms, 1 bath
- Basement foundation

Special features

- 1,705 total square feet of living area
- Cozy design includes two bedrooms on the first floor and two bedrooms on the second floor for added privacy
- L-shaped kitchen provides easy access to the dining room and the outdoors
- Convenient first floor laundry area
- 2" x 6" exterior walls available, please order plan #598-001D-0111
- 4 bedrooms, 2 baths
- Crawl space foundation, drawings also include basement and slab foundations

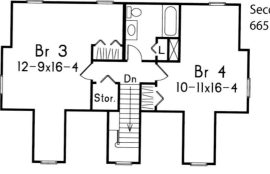

Second Floor
665 sq. ft.

Br 3
12-9x16-4

Br 4
10-11x16-4

Stor.

Dn

L

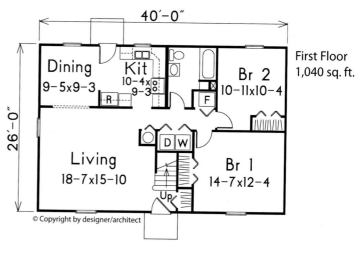

40'-0"

26'-0"

Dining
9-5x9-3

Kit
10-4x
9-3

Br 2
10-11x10-4

Living
18-7x15-10

Br 1
14-7x12-4

D W

R

F

Up

First Floor
1,040 sq. ft.

© Copyright by designer/architect

Rear Elevation

Second Floor
1,222 sq. ft.

VAULTED
MASTER
13/8 X 12/0

BONUS
14/6 X 18/0 •
(9' CLG.)

BR. 2
11/4 X 10/0

DN.

BR. 3
11/4 X 11/0

LIN.

© Copyright by
designer/architect

NOOK
9/6 X 10/0
(9' CLG.)

3RD CAR/
STOR.
9/8 X 18/8

GREAT RM.
19/0 X 15/8
(9' CLG.)

REF.

PAN.

DINING
11/8 X 11/8
(9' CLG.)

GARAGE
19/8 X 20/8

BUILT-INS

STUDY
11/6 X 10/0
(9' CLG.)

UP

PORCH

40'

52'

First Floor
1,082 sq. ft.

Special features

- 2,304 total square feet of living area
- Energy efficient home with 2" x 6" exterior walls
- Private study is furnished with built-in storage
- Impressive columns define the dining room
- Master suite has a vaulted ceiling, private bath and corner tub
- Bonus room on the second floor is included in the square footage
- 3 bedrooms, 2 1/2 baths, 3-car garage
- Crawl space foundation

Special features

- 1,085 total square feet of living area
- Rear porch provides handy access through the kitchen
- Convenient hall linen closet is located on the second floor
- Breakfast bar in the kitchen offers additional counterspace
- Living and dining rooms combine for open living
- 3 bedrooms, 2 baths
- Basement foundation

Rear Elevation

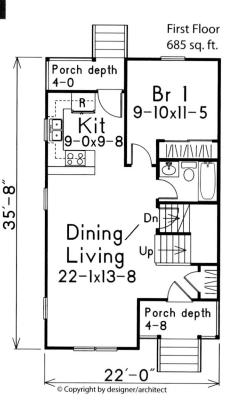

Porch depth
4-0

R

Kit
9-0x9-8

First Floor
685 sq. ft.

Br 1
9-10x11-5

35'-8"

Dining/
Living
22-1x13-8

Dn

Up

Porch depth
4-8

22'-0"

© Copyright by designer/architect

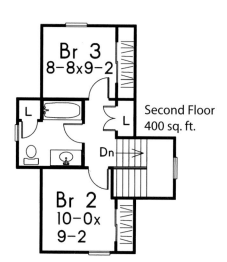

Br 3
8-8x9-2

L

L

Second Floor
400 sq. ft.

Dn

Br 2
10-0x
9-2

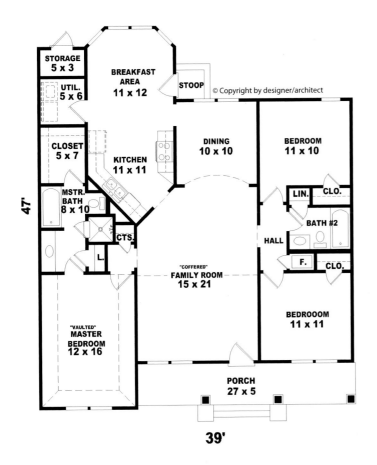

STORAGE
5 x 3

UTIL.
5 x 6

BREAKFAST
AREA
11 x 12

STOOP

© Copyright by designer/architect

CLOSET
5 x 7

KITCHEN
11 x 11

DINING
10 x 10

BEDROOM
11 x 10

MSTR.
BATH
8 x 10

CTS.

L.

LIN.

CLO.

BATH #2

HALL

F.

CLO.

"COFFERED"
FAMILY ROOM
15 x 21

"VAULTED"
MASTER
BEDROOM
12 x 16

BEDROOOM
11 x 11

47'

PORCH
27 x 5

39'

Special features

- 1,437 total square feet of living area
- The covered front porch opens into the massive family room
- The private master bedroom enjoys a vaulted ceiling, dressing area and bath with walk-in closet
- Two secondary bedrooms are located in a separate wing and share a full bath
- 3 bedrooms, 2 baths
- Slab foundation

Special features

- 835 total square feet of living area
- Energy efficient home with 2" x 6" exterior walls
- Cozy porch greets guests
- An open floor plan dominates the first floor including the living/dining area and kitchen
- U-shaped kitchen boasts a lengthy breakfast counter
- A gas stove warms the entire living area
- The second floor loft adds flexibility to this plan
- 1 bedroom, 1 bath
- Crawl space foundation

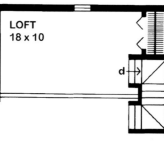

LOFT
18 x 10

d →

Second Floor
240 sq. ft.

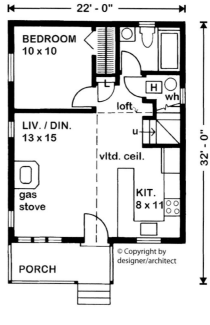

|← 22' - 0" →|

BEDROOM
10 x 10

loft

LIV. / DIN.
13 x 15

vltd. ceil.

gas stove

KIT.
8 x 11

H wh

u

First Floor
595 sq. ft.

32' - 0"

PORCH

First Floor
1,713 sq. ft.

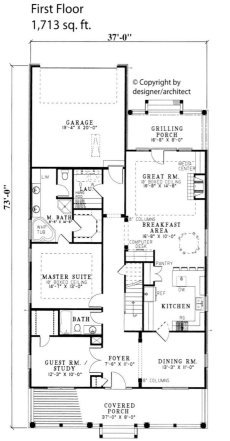

© Copyright by
designer/architect

37'-0"

73'-0"

GARAGE
19'-4" X 20'-0"

GRILLING
PORCH
16'-8" X 8'-0"

MEDIA
CENTER

LAU

M. BATH
8'-8" X 14'-8"

WHP
TUB

GREAT RM.
10' BOXED CEILING
16'-8" X 14'-8"

8' COLUMNS

BREAKFAST
AREA
16'-8" X 10'-0"

COMPUTER
DESK

MASTER SUITE
10' BOXED CEILING
14'-7" X 13'-0"

PANTRY

REF   DW

KITCHEN

BATH

UP

RG

GUEST RM. /
STUDY
12'-3" X 10'-0"

FOYER
7'-6" X 11'-0"

DINING RM.
13'-3" X 11'-0"

8' COLUMNS

COVERED
PORCH
37'-0" X 8'-0"

Second Floor
994 sq. ft.

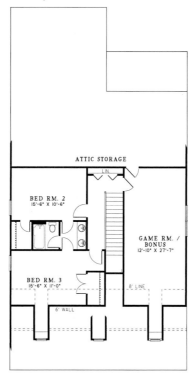

ATTIC STORAGE

LIN.

BED RM. 2
15'-6" X 10'-6"

GAME RM. /
BONUS
12'-10" X 27'-7"

BED RM. 3
15'-6" X 11'-0"

8' LINE

6' WALL

Special features

- 2,707 total square feet of living area
- A double-door entry leads into a handsome study
- Kitchen and breakfast room flow into the great room creating a terrific gathering place
- The second floor includes a game room/bonus room which is included in the total square footage
- 4 bedrooms, 3 baths, 2-car rear entry garage
- Crawl space or slab foundation, please specify when ordering

Special features

- 1,818 total square feet of living area
- Spacious living and dining rooms
- Master bedroom has a walk-in closet, dressing area and bath
- Convenient carport and storage area
- 2" x 6" exterior walls available, please order plan #598-001D-0113
- 3 bedrooms, 2 1/2 baths, 1-car carport
- Crawl space foundation, drawings also include basement and slab foundations

Rear Elevation

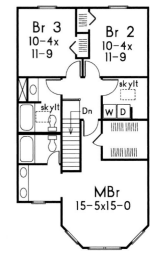

Patio

Living
23-5x15-8
raised ceiling

© Copyright by designer/architect

Storage

L Furn

Kit
12-3x
12-2

Carport

R

Foyer

Up

42'-0"

Dining
15-5x13-0

Porch depth 6-0

36'-0"

First Floor
928 sq. ft.

Second Floor
890 sq. ft.

Br 3
10-4x
11-9

Br 2
10-4x
11-9

skylt

skylt

Dn

W D

MBr
15-5x15-0

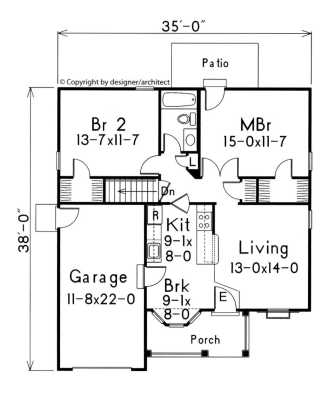

35'-0"

Patio

© Copyright by designer/architect

Br 2
13-7x11-7

MBr
15-0x11-7

38'-0"

Dn

R

Kit
9-1x
8-0

Living
13-0x14-0

Garage
11-8x22-0

Brk
9-1x
8-0

E

Porch

Special features

- 888 total square feet of living area
- Home features an eye-catching exterior and has a spacious porch
- The breakfast room with bay window is open to the living room and adjoins the kitchen with pass-through snack bar
- The bedrooms are quite roomy and feature walk-in closets
- The master bedroom has a double-door entry and access to the rear patio
- 2 bedrooms, 1 bath, 1-car garage
- Basement foundation

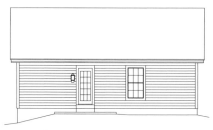

Rear Elevation

Special features

- ■ 1,245 total square feet of living area
- ■ Energy efficient home with 2" x 6" exterior walls
- ■ Master bedroom has a reading area and private balcony
- ■ Bay window brightens living area
- ■ Combined laundry area and half bath
- ■ 3 bedrooms, 1 1/2 baths
- ■ Basement foundation

First Floor
626 sq. ft.

Second Floor
619 sq. ft.

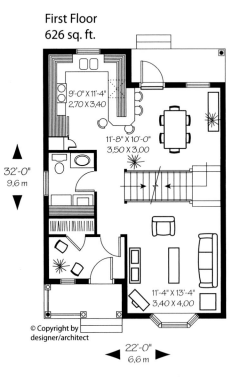

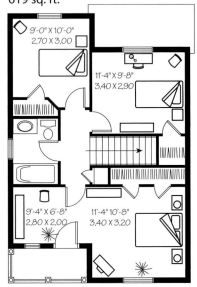

9'-0" X 11'-4"
2,70 X 3,40

11'-8" X 10'-0"
3,50 X 3,00

11'-4" X 13'-4"
3,40 X 4,00

9'-0" X 10'-0"
2,70 X 3,00

11'-4" X 9'-8"
3,40 X 2,90

9'-4" X 6'-8"
2,80 X 2,00

11'-4" 10'-8"
3,40 X 3,20

32'-0"
9,6 m

22'-0"
6,6 m

Special features

- 1,617 total square feet of living area
- Kitchen and breakfast area overlook the great room with fireplace
- Formal dining room features a vaulted ceiling and an elegant circle-top window
- All bedrooms are located on the second floor for privacy
- 3 bedrooms, 2 1/2 baths, 2-car garage
- Partial crawl space/slab foundation

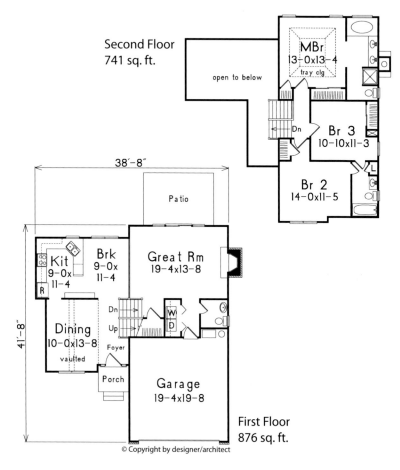

Second Floor
741 sq. ft.

open to below

MBr
13-0x13-4
tray clg

Dn

Br 3
10-10x11-3

Br 2
14-0x11-5

38'-8"

Patio

41'-8"

Kit
9-0x11-4

Brk
9-0x11-4

Great Rm
19-4x13-8

Dn

W D

Up

Dining
10-0x13-8
vaulted

Foyer

Porch

Garage
19-4x19-8

First Floor
876 sq. ft.

© Copyright by designer/architect

Rear Elevation

Special features

- 1,880 total square feet of living area
- Master bedroom is enhanced with a coffered ceiling
- Generous family and breakfast areas are modern and functional
- The front porch complements the front facade
- 3 bedrooms, 2 1/2 baths, 2-car drive under garage
- Basement foundation

Rear Elevation

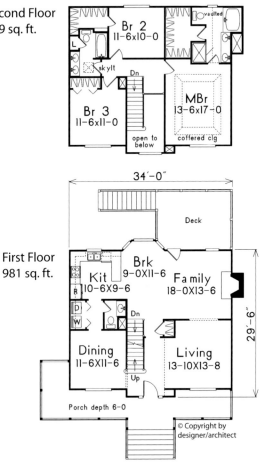

Second Floor
899 sq. ft.

Br 2
11-6x10-0

vaulted

L

skylt

Dn

MBr
13-6x17-0

Br 3
11-6x11-0

open to below

coffered clg

First Floor
981 sq. ft.

34'-0"

Deck

Brk
9-0x11-6

Kit
10-6X9-6

Family
18-0X13-6

R

29'-6"

D
W

Dn

Dining
11-6X11-6

Up

Living
13-10X13-8

Porch depth 6-0

Second Floor
615 sq. ft.

Bedroom
12-0x11-0

L

Dn

Shel.

Living Rm
14-0x13-0

R

Kitchen
6-4x11-0

DW

Special features

■ 615 total square feet of living area

■ The exterior includes a front porch and upper gabled box windows

■ The first floor features an oversized two-car garage with built-in storage shelves and a mechanical room

■ A large living room with fireplace, entertainment alcove and kitchen open to an eating area are just a few of the many features of the second floor

■ 1 bedroom, 1 bath, 2-car garage

■ Slab foundation

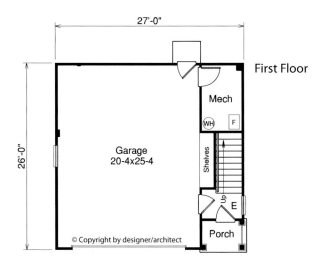

27'-0"

First Floor

Mech

WH   F

Garage
20-4x25-4

Shelves

26'-0"

Up   E

Porch

© Copyright by designer/architect

Rear Elevation

Special features

- 920 total square feet of living area
- Energy efficient home with 2" x 6" exterior walls
- The bath has extra space for a washer and dryer
- Plenty of seating is available for dining at the kitchen counter
- 2 bedrooms, 1 bath
- Basement foundation

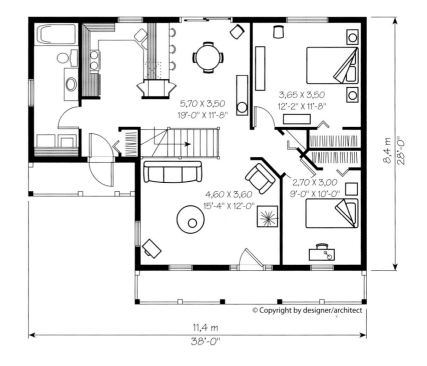

5,70 X 3,50
19'-0" X 11'-8"

3,65 X 3,50
12'-2" X 11'-8"

4,60 X 3,60
15'-4" X 12'-0"

2,70 X 3,00
9'-0" X 10'-0"

8,4 m
28'-0"

11,4 m
38'-0"

© Copyright by designer/architect

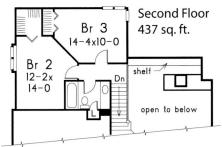

Second Floor
437 sq. ft.

Br 3
14-4x10-0

Br 2
12-2x
14-0

shelf

Dn

open to below

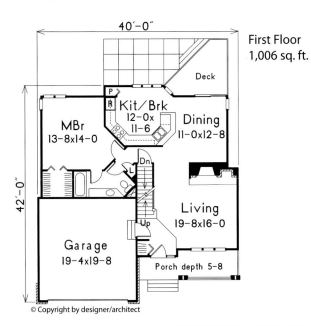

40'-0"

Deck

Kit/Brk
12-0x
11-6

Dining
11-0x12-8

MBr
13-8x14-0

42'-0"

Dn

L

Living
19-8x16-0

Up

Garage
19-4x19-8

Porch depth 5-8

First Floor
1,006 sq. ft.

Special features

- 1,443 total square feet of living area
- A raised foyer and a cathedral ceiling in the living room add character to the interior
- Impressive tall-wall fireplace between the living and dining rooms
- Open U-shaped kitchen features a cheerful breakfast bay
- Angular side deck accentuates patio and garden
- First floor master bedroom has a walk-in closet and a corner window
- 3 bedrooms, 2 baths, 2-car garage
- Basement foundation

Rear Elevation

Special features

- 2,058 total square feet of living area
- Designed for today's more narrow lots, this home adds style to any neighborhood
- All bedrooms are located on the second floor but are easily accessible thanks to a centrally located elevator
- The dramatic and spacious kitchen flows neatly from an angled pantry to the recipe desk and serving bar
- 3 bedrooms, 2 1/2 baths, 2-car garage
- Slab or crawl space foundation, please specify when ordering

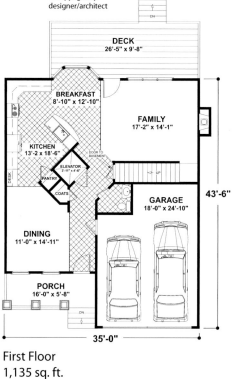

© Copyright by designer/architect

DECK
26'-5" x 9'-8"

BREAKFAST
8'-10" x 12'-10"

FAMILY
17'-2" x 14'-1"

KITCHEN
13'-2 x 18'-6"

DOOR TO BASEMENT

ELEVATOR
3'-11" x 4'-4"

PANTRY

COATS

DESK

UP

GARAGE
18'-0" x 24'-10"

DINING
11'-0" x 14'-11"

43'-6"

PORCH
16'-0" x 5'-8"

DN

35'-0"

First Floor
1,135 sq. ft.

BEDROOM 3
12'-4" x 11'-4"

VAULT

HERS

VAULT

ELEVATOR

LINEN

BEDROOM 2
11'-0" x 15'-6"

LAUNDRY
8'-1" x 5'-0"

MASTER SUITE
14'-6" x 15'-4"

HIS

TRAY CEILING

SITTING
7'-0" x 9'-2"

Second Floor
923 sq. ft.

Rear View

Special features

- 987 total square feet of living area
- Galley kitchen opens into the cozy breakfast room
- Convenient coat closets are located by both entrances
- Dining/living room offers an expansive open area
- Breakfast room has access to the outdoors
- Front porch is great for enjoying outdoor living
- 3 bedrooms, 1 bath
- Basement foundation

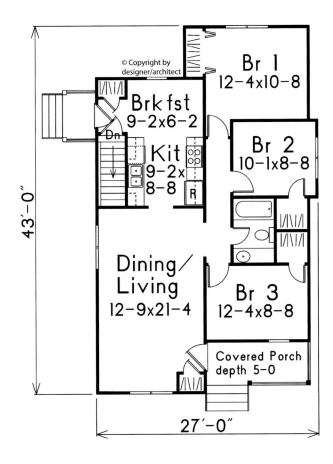

© Copyright by designer/architect

Br 1
12-4x10-8

Brk fst
9-2x6-2

Dn

Kit
9-2x
8-8

Br 2
10-1x8-8

43'-0"

Dining/
Living
12-9x21-4

Br 3
12-4x8-8

Covered Porch
depth 5-0

27'-0"

Rear Elevation

Special features

- 1,902 total square feet of living area
- Energy efficient home with 2" x 6" exterior walls
- A two-story great room is stunning with a fireplace and many windows
- Breakfast nook and kitchen combine creating a warm and inviting place to dine
- Second floor hall overlooks to great room below
- Bonus room on the second floor is included in the square footage
- 3 bedrooms, 2 1/2 baths, 2-car garage
- Crawl space foundation

Second Floor
672 sq. ft.

BR. 3
12/6 X 12/2 +/-

BR. 2
10/9 X 12/2 +/-

LIN

BONUS RM.
13/6 X 12/6

OPEN TO
GREAT RM.
BELOW

DN.

ATTIC
STORAGE

First Floor
1,230 sq. ft.

NOOK
8/8 X 8/10

DINING
9/10 X 10/4

VAULTED
MASTER
16/0 X 11/10

REF

LINEN

SPA

TWO STORY
GREAT RM.
15/10 X 19/8

D W

UP

GARAGE
19/4 X 21/8

© Copyright by
designer/architect

◄ 40' ►

53'

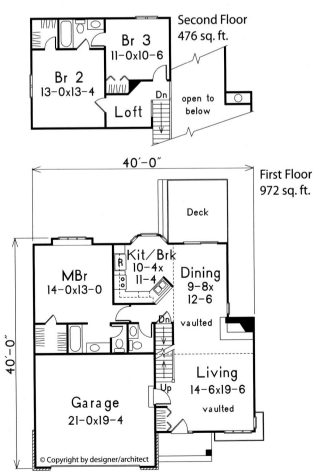

Second Floor
476 sq. ft.

Br 3
11-0x10-6

Br 2
13-0x13-4

Loft

Dn

open to below

40'-0"

First Floor
972 sq. ft.

40'-0"

Deck

Kit/Brk
10-4x
11-4

Dining
9-8x
12-6

MBr
14-0x13-0

Dn   vaulted

Up

Living
14-6x19-6
vaulted

Garage
21-0x19-4

© Copyright by designer/architect

Special features

- 1,448 total square feet of living area
- Dining room conveniently adjoins kitchen and accesses rear deck
- Private first floor master bedroom
- Secondary bedrooms share a bath and cozy loft area
- 3 bedrooms, 2 1/2 baths, 2-car garage
- Basement foundation

Rear Elevation

Special features

- 2,565 total square feet of living area
- Large master suite includes access to the outdoors and has double walk-in closets and a spa-style tub
- Efficiently designed kitchen has a center island ideal for food preparation and a large pantry for storage
- 10' ceilings throughout first floor provide added openness
- 3 bedrooms, 3 baths, 2-car side entry garage
- Slab foundation

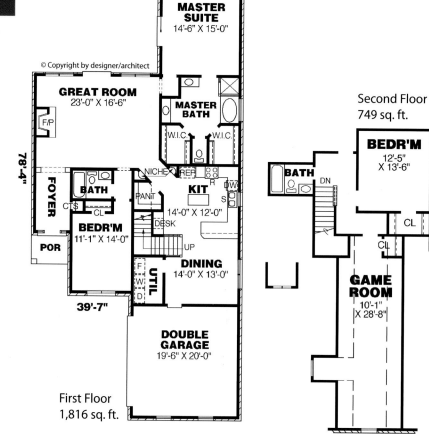

MASTER SUITE 14'-6" X 15'-0"

GREAT ROOM 23'-0" X 16'-6"

F/P

MASTER BATH

W.I.C. W.I.C.

FOYER

BATH

CT$ CL

NICHE REF

KIT 14'-0" X 12'-0"

DW R S

PANT

DESK

BEDR'M 11'-1" X 14'-0"

UP

POR

F W D

UTIL

DINING 14'-0" X 13'-0"

78'-4"

39'-7"

DOUBLE GARAGE 19'-6" X 20'-0"

First Floor 1,816 sq. ft.

Second Floor 749 sq. ft.

BATH

DN

BEDR'M 12'-5" X 13'-6"

CL

CL

GAME ROOM 10'-1" X 28'-8"

Special features

- 882 total square feet of living area
- An inviting porch and entry lure you into this warm and cozy home
- Living room features a vaulted ceiling, bayed dining area and is open to a well-equipped U-shaped kitchen
- The master bedroom has two separate closets and an access door to the rear patio
- 2 bedrooms, 1 bath
- Crawl space foundation, drawings also include slab and basement foundations

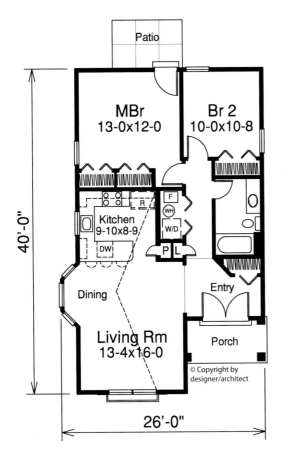

Patio

MBr
13-0x12-0

Br 2
10-0x10-8

40'-0"

F
WH
W/D
P L

Kitchen
9-10x8-9

DW

Dining

Entry

Living Rm
13-4x16-0

Porch

© Copyright by
designer/architect

26'-0"

Rear Elevation

Special features

- 1,693 total square feet of living area
- This home is designed for a narrow lot without compromising space for family living
- A lovely four season room offers the feeling of year-round outdoor enjoyment while remaining indoors
- A double-door entry makes the den private and secluded, perfect as a home office
- 2 bedrooms, 2 baths, 2-car side entry garage
- Basement foundation

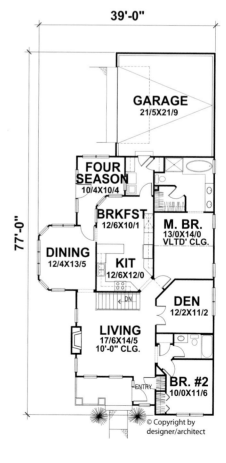

39'-0"

77'-0"

GARAGE
21/5X21/9

FOUR SEASON
10/4X10/4

BRKFST
12/6X10/1

M. BR.
13/0X14/0
VLTD' CLG.

DINING
12/4X13/5

KIT
12/6X12/0

DN

DEN
12/2X11/2

LIVING
17/6X14/5
10'-0" CLG.

BR. #2
10/0X11/6

ENTRY

© Copyright by designer/architect

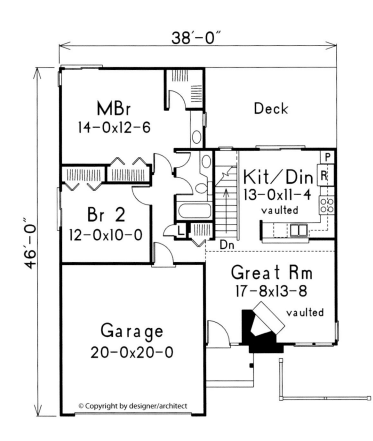

38'-0"

MBr
14-0x12-6

Deck

Br 2
12-0x10-0

Kit/Din
13-0x11-4
vaulted

P

R

46'-0"

Dn

Great Rm
17-8x13-8
vaulted

Garage
20-0x20-0

© Copyright by designer/architect

Special features

- 988 total square feet of living area
- Great room features a corner fireplace
- Vaulted ceiling and corner windows add space and light in great room
- Eat-in kitchen with vaulted ceiling accesses deck for outdoor living
- Master bedroom features separate vanities and private access to the bath
- 2 bedrooms, 1 bath, 2-car garage
- Basement foundation

Rear Elevation

Special features

- 986 total square feet of living area
- Wide and tall windows in the kitchen, dining and living areas create bright and cheerful spaces
- Three bedrooms with plenty of closet space and an oversized hall bath are located at the rear of the home
- An extra-deep garage has storage space at the rear and access to the patio behind the garage
- Convenient linen closet is located in the hall
- 3 bedrooms, 1 bath, 1-car garage
- Basement foundation, drawings also include crawl space and slab foundations

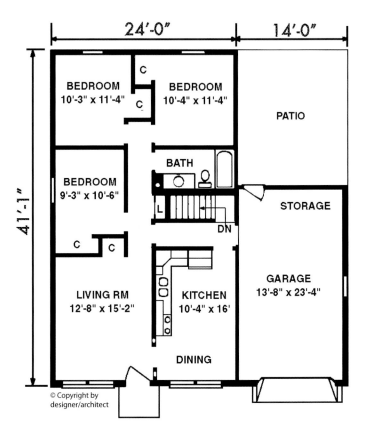

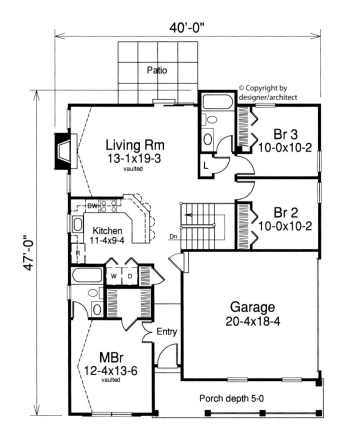

40'-0"

Patio

© Copyright by
designer/architect

Living Rm
13-1x19-3
vaulted

Br 3
10-0x10-2

Kitchen
11-4x9-4

DW

L

Br 2
10-0x10-2

Dn

47'-0"

W   D

Garage
20-4x18-4

Entry

MBr
12-4x13-6
vaulted

Porch depth 5-0

Special features

- 1,202 total square feet of living area
- All the necessary ingredients provided in a simple structure that's affordable to build
- The vaulted living room features a fireplace, dining area and access to the rear patio
- An angled snack bar is the highlight of this well-planned U-shaped kitchen
- 3 bedrooms, 2 baths, 2-car side entry garage
- Basement foundation, drawings also include slab and crawl space foundations

Rear Elevation

Special features

- 1,270 total square feet of living area
- Spacious living area features angled stairs, vaulted ceiling, exciting fireplace and deck access
- Master bedroom includes a walk-in closet and private bath
- Dining and living rooms join to create an open atmosphere
- Eat-in kitchen has a convenient pass-through to the dining room
- 3 bedrooms, 2 baths, 2-car garage
- Basement foundation

Rear Elevation

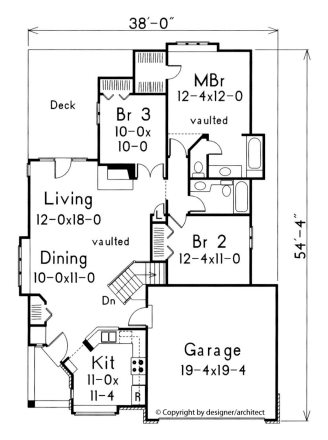

38'-0"

54'-4"

Deck

MBr
12-4x12-0
vaulted

Br 3
10-0x
10-0

Living
12-0x18-0
vaulted

Br 2
12-4x11-0

Dining
10-0x11-0

Dn

Kit
11-0x
11-4

Garage
19-4x19-4

© Copyright by designer/architect

Special features

- 1,107 total square feet of living area
- L-shaped kitchen has a serving bar overlooking the dining/living room
- Second floor bedrooms share a bath with the linen closet
- Front porch opens into the foyer with convenient coat closet
- 3 bedrooms, 2 baths
- Basement foundation

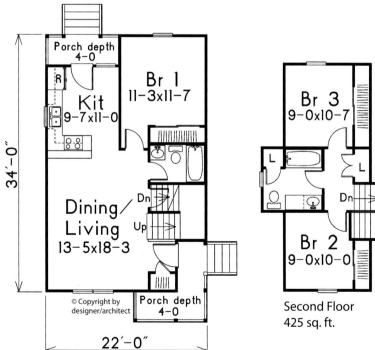

Porch depth 4-0

R

Kit
9-7x11-0

Br 1
11-3x11-7

34'-0"

Dining
Living
13-5x18-3

Dn

Up

© Copyright by designer/architect

Porch depth 4-0

22'-0"

First Floor
682 sq. ft.

Br 3
9-0x10-7

L

L

Dn

Br 2
9-0x10-0

Second Floor
425 sq. ft.

Rear Elevation

Special features

- 1,299 total square feet of living area
- Large porch for enjoying relaxing evenings
- First floor master bedroom has a bay window, walk-in closet and roomy bath
- Two generous bedrooms with lots of closet space, a hall bath, linen closet and balcony overlook comprise the second floor
- 3 bedrooms, 2 1/2 baths
- Basement foundation

Rear Elevation

24'-0"

Patio

© Copyright by designer/architect

P
R

Kit
12-0x14-10

MBr
13-0x13-6

40'-0"

Dn

Living Rm
12-1x18-3

Up
L

L

Porch depth 6-0

First Floor
834 sq. ft.

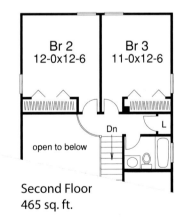

Br 2
12-0x12-6

Br 3
11-0x12-6

Dn
L

open to below

Second Floor
465 sq. ft.

20'

© Copyright by designer/architect

SUNDECK

8'

GREAT ROOM
19' X 14'
VAULTED CEILING

28'

UP

KIT
11' x 10'

4'

COVERED PORCH

First Floor
560 sq. ft.

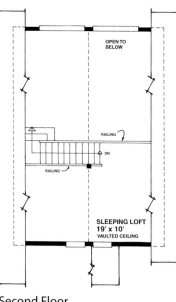

OPEN TO
BELOW

RAILING

DN

RAILING

SLEEPING LOFT
19' X 10'
VAULTED CEILING

Second Floor
236 sq. ft.

Special features

- 796 total square feet of living area
- Energy efficient home with 2" x 6" exterior walls
- This home is perfect for a narrow lot
- The second floor sleeping loft has the ability to be partitioned for additional privacy
- The covered front entry is protected from the elements and adds to the curb appeal
- 1 bedroom, 1 bath
- Crawl space foundation

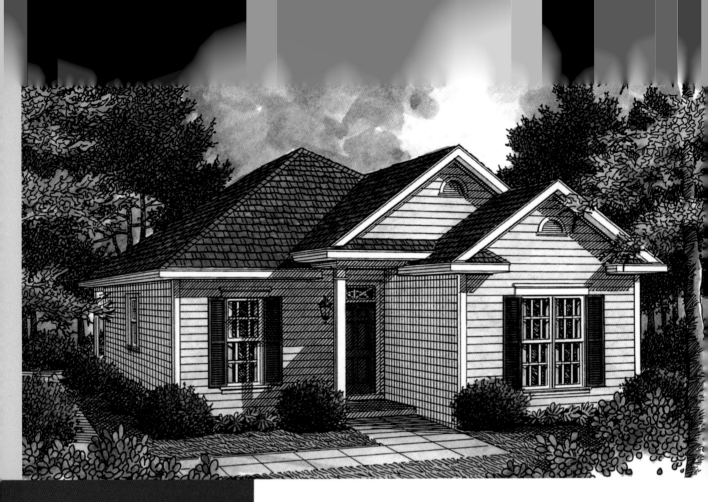

Special features

- 1,401 total square feet of living area
- This home is perfect for tackling a narrow lot
- The bedrooms share the right side of the home and are private from the living areas
- A corner fireplace in the family room also warms the adjoining kitchen and dining room
- Sliding glass doors lead to the relaxing rear porch
- 3 bedrooms, 2 baths
- Slab foundation

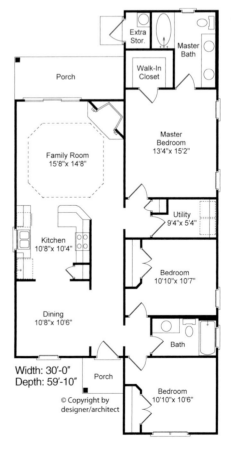

Extra Stor.

Master Bath

Porch

Walk-In Closet

Master Bedroom
13'4"x 15'2"

Family Room
15'8"x 14'8"

Utility
9'4"x 5'4"

Kitchen
10'8"x 10'4"

Bedroom
10'10"x 10'7"

Dining
10'8"x 10'6"

Bath

Width: 30'-0"
Depth: 59'-10"

Porch

Bedroom
10'10"x 10'6"

© Copyright by
designer/architect

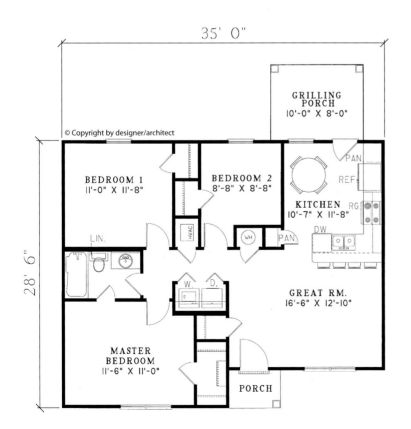

35' 0"

28' 6"

© Copyright by designer/architect

GRILLING PORCH
10'-0" X 8'-0"

BEDROOM 1
11'-0" X 11'-8"

BEDROOM 2
8'-8" X 8'-8"

KITCHEN
10'-7" X 11'-8"

PAN

REF.

RG

DW

HVAC

WH

PAN

LIN.

W D.

GREAT RM.
16'-6" X 12'-10"

MASTER BEDROOM
11'-6" X 11'-0"

PORCH

Special features

- 930 total square feet of living area
- Kitchen overlooks the great room and includes space for counter dining
- Convenient laundry closet
- Master bedroom has walk-in closet and direct access to hall bath
- 3 bedrooms, 1 bath
- Slab or crawl space foundation, please specify when ordering

Special features

- 2,207 total square feet of living area
- This home is designed perfectly for a narrow lot
- A cheerful breakfast room enjoys a bay window adding warmth and light to the entire space
- All the bedrooms are located on the second floor for privacy and seclusion from everyday activity
- 3 bedrooms, 2 1/2 baths, 2-car side entry garage
- Basement foundation

38'-0"

© Copyright by designer/architect

GARAGE
21/9X21/5

First Floor
1,232 sq. ft.

76'-8"

PATIO

SUN RM.
12/9X11/5

Second Floor
975 sq. ft.

KIT
13/8X16/8

BRKFST
11/3X10/11
TRAY CLG.

DINING
14/5X13/5

BR. #3
12/1X12/0

BR. #2
10/5X10/10

DN

UP

DN

ENTRY

LIVING
14/5X14/5

M. BR.
14/5X17/4
COFFERED CLG.

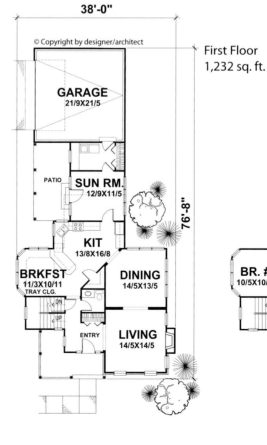

Special features

- 1,500 total square feet of living area
- Energy efficient home with 2" x 6" exterior walls
- Kitchen and dining area are perfectly organized with a center island, large pantry and work desk
- Vaulted master bedroom has its own bath
- A plant shelf graces the foyer
- 3 bedrooms, 2 1/2 baths, 2-car garage
- Crawl space foundation

DINING
11/4 X 12/6

2 STORY
GREAT RM.
13/6 X 16/6 +/-

10/2 X 12/6

REF

DESK

PANTRY

STOR

UP

GARAGE
21/0 X 21/6

44'

◀ 36' ▶

First Floor
716 sq. ft.

VAULTED
MASTER
11/8 X 14/4

GREAT RM.
BELOW

DN

LINEN

FOYER
BELOW

PLANT SHELF

BR. 2
10/4 X 13/4 +/-

BR. 3
10/4 X 11/0 +

Second Floor
784 sq. ft.

Special features

- 1,000 total square feet of living area
- Master bedroom has double closets and an adjacent bath
- L-shaped kitchen includes side entrance, closet and convenient laundry area
- Living room features handy coat closet
- 3 bedrooms, 1 bath
- Crawl space foundation, drawings also include basement and slab foundations

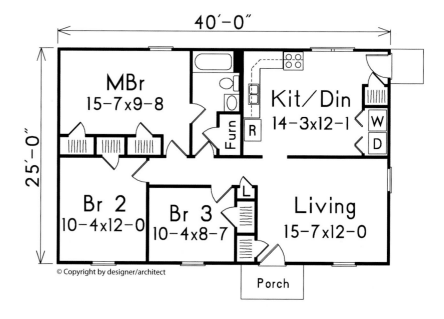

40'-0"

25'-0"

MBr
15-7x9-8

Kit/Din
14-3x12-1

Furn

R

W

D

Br 2
10-4x12-0

Br 3
10-4x8-7

L

Living
15-7x12-0

Porch

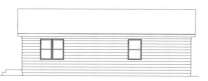

Rear Elevation

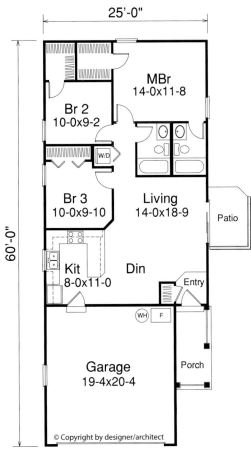

25'-0"

MBr
14-0x11-8

Br 2
10-0x9-2

W/D

Br 3
10-0x9-10

Living
14-0x18-9

Patio

60'-0"

Kit
8-0x11-0

Din

Entry

WH F

Garage
19-4x20-4

Porch

© Copyright by designer/architect

Special features

- 983 total square feet of living area
- Spacious front porch leads you into the living and dining areas open to a pass-through kitchen
- A small patio with privacy fence creates exterior access from the living room
- The master bedroom includes a large walk-in closet and its own private full bath
- 3 bedrooms, 2 baths, 2-car garage
- Crawl space foundation, drawings also include slab foundation

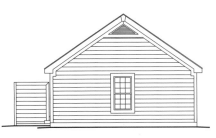

Rear Elevation

Special features

- 1,123 total square feet of living area
- Spacious kitchen and breakfast area feature vaulted ceilings and patio access
- Fireplace warms the adjoining family and dining rooms
- Secondary bedrooms are secluded and share a bath
- 3 bedrooms, 2 baths, 1-car garage
- Crawl space or slab foundation, please specify when ordering

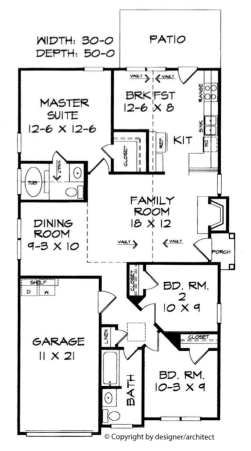

WIDTH: 30-0
DEPTH: 50-0

PATIO

MASTER SUITE
12-6 X 12-6

BRK FST
12-6 X 8

KIT

DINING ROOM
9-3 X 10

FAMILY ROOM
18 X 12

PORCH

GARAGE
11 X 21

BD. RM. 2
10 X 9

BATH

BD. RM.
10-3 X 9

Special features

- 858 total square feet of living area
- Stackable washer/dryer is located in the kitchen
- Large covered porch graces this exterior
- Both bedrooms have walk-in closets
- 2 bedrooms, 1 bath
- Crawl space foundation

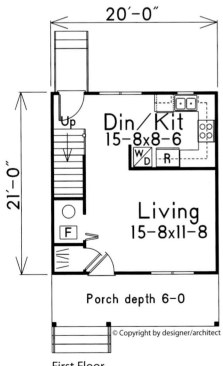

20'-0"

21'-0"

Up

Din/Kit
15-8x8-6

W D R

Living
15-8x11-8

F

Porch depth 6-0

© Copyright by designer/architect

First Floor
420 sq. ft.

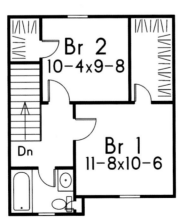

Br 2
10-4x9-8

Dn

Br 1
11-8x10-6

Second Floor
438 sq. ft.

Rear Elevation

Special features

- 1,565 total square feet of living area
- Centrally located master bedroom is convenient
- Vaulted ceilings are found throughout this home
- Well-organized kitchen has a convenient pantry and utility closets
- Framing - only concrete block available
- 3 bedrooms, 2 baths, 2-car garage
- Slab foundation

Family Room
vaulted ceiling
14^4 · 13^{10}

Master Bedroom
vaulted ceiling
15^2 · 12^4

Bath

w.i.c.   lin

Kitchen

dw

ref   pan

vaulted ceiling

opt.

Breakfast

Living Room

vaulted ceiling
19^4 · 16^0

Bedroom 2
vaulted ceiling
12^0 · 10^0

Dining

Bath

lin

Utility

d   w

wh   ac   Foyer

opt.

Bedroom 3
vaulted ceiling
12^0 · 10^4

Double Garage

Entry

© Copyright by designer/architect

Width: 40'-0"
Depth: 55'-0"

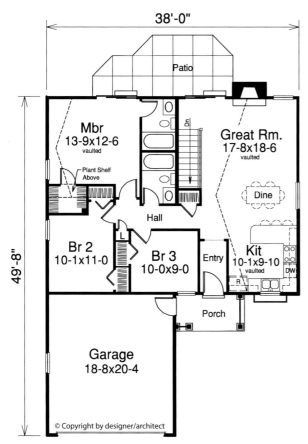

38'-0"

Patio

Mbr
13-9x12-6
vaulted

Plant Shelf
Above

Great Rm.
17-8x18-6
vaulted

Dn

Dine

Hall

49'-8"

Br 2
10-1x11-0

Br 3
10-0x9-0

Entry

Kit
10-1x9-10
vaulted

DW

R

Porch

Garage
18-8x20-4

© Copyright by designer/architect

Special features

- 1,102 total square feet of living area
- Attractive exterior features a cozy porch, palladian windows and a decorative planter box
- The vaulted great room has a fireplace and view to rear patio
- Open to the great room is a U-shaped kitchen which includes all the necessities and a breakfast bar
- The master bedroom offers a vaulted ceiling, private bath, walk-in closet and sliding doors to the patio
- 3 bedrooms, 2 baths, 2-car garage
- Basement foundation, drawings also include slab and crawl space foundations

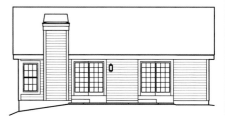

Rear Elevation

Special features

- 2,613 total square feet of living area
- Second floor loft space would make an ideal sitting area for the master suite
- Open kitchen flows into breakfast room
- A spacious dining room is provided for entertaining
- 3 bedrooms, 2 baths
- Slab foundation

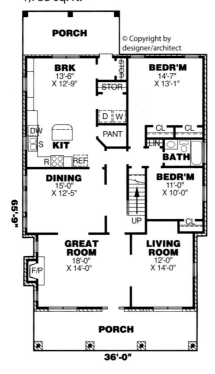

First Floor
1,733 sq. ft.

© Copyright by
designer/architect

PORCH

BRK
13'-6"
X 12'-9"

STOR

D   W

PANT

BEDR'M
14'-7"
X 13'-1"

CL   CL

LIN

BATH

DW
S

KIT

R   REF

DINING
15'-0"
X 12'-5"

UP

BEDR'M
11'-0"
X 10'-0"

CL

65'-9"

GREAT
ROOM
18'-0"
X 14'-0"

F/P

LIVING
ROOM
12'-0"
X 14'-0"

PORCH

36'-0"

Second Floor
880 sq. ft.

CL

LOFT

MASTER
BATH

BALCONY

GLASS
SHOWER

CL

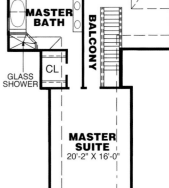

MASTER
SUITE
20'-2" X 16'-0"

Special features

- 1,067 total square feet of living area
- The U-shaped kitchen opens into the cozy dining area and includes access to the rear patio to extend mealtime opportunities
- Coffered ceilings enhance the family area and master bedroom
- The home includes a convenient storage closet located at the rear of the home
- 3 bedrooms, 2 baths
- Slab foundation

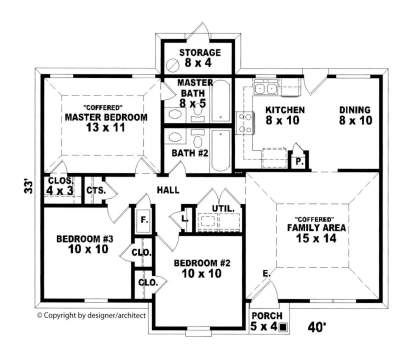

STORAGE
8 x 4

MASTER
BATH
8 x 5

"COFFERED"
MASTER BEDROOM
13 x 11

KITCHEN
8 x 10

DINING
8 x 10

BATH #2

CLOS.
4 x 3

CTS.

HALL

UTIL.

"COFFERED"
FAMILY AREA
15 x 14

F.

L

33'

BEDROOM #3
10 x 10

CLO.

BEDROOM #2
10 x 10

E.

CLO.

PORCH
5 x 4

40'

Special features

- 576 total square feet of living area
- Perfect country retreat features vaulted living room and entry with skylights and a plant shelf above
- A double-door entry leads to the vaulted bedroom with bath access
- Kitchen offers generous storage and a pass-through breakfast bar
- 1 bedroom, 1 bath
- Crawl space foundation

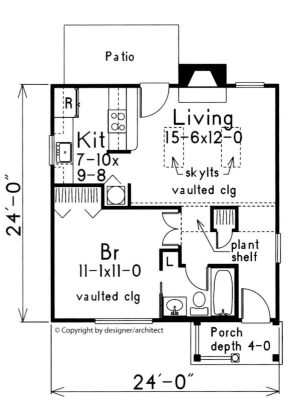

Patio

Living
15-6x12-0
skylts
vaulted clg

Kit
7-10x
9-8

plant shelf

Br
11-1x11-0
vaulted clg

L

R

24'-0"

24'-0"

Porch
depth 4-0

Rear Elevation

Special features

- 1,805 total square feet of living area
- Energy efficient home with 2" x 6" exterior walls
- Cooktop island, a handy desk and dining area make the kitchen highly functional
- Open floor plan with tall ceilings creates an airy atmosphere
- Family and living rooms are both enhanced with fireplaces
- 3 bedrooms, 2 1/2 baths, 2-car garage
- Crawl space foundation

First Floor
968 sq. ft.

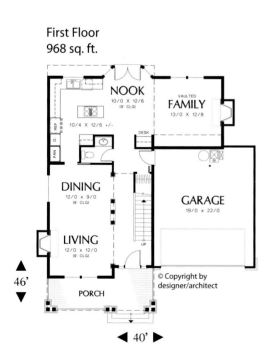

NOOK
10/0 X 12/6
(9' CLG)

VAULTED
FAMILY
13/0 X 12/8

10/4 X 12/6 +/-

PAN

REF

DESK

DINING
12/0 x 9/0
(9' CLG)

GARAGE
19/0 x 22/0

UP

LIVING
12/0 x 12/0
(9' CLG)

PORCH

© Copyright by
designer/architect

46'

40'

Second Floor
837 sq. ft.

VAULTED
MASTER
13/0 X 12/6

LINEN

DN

BR. 3
10/8 x 11/0

D W

BR. 2
12/0 X 10/0

Special features

- 1,643 total square feet of living area
- First floor master bedroom has a private bath, walk-in closet and easy access to the laundry closet
- Comfortable family room features a vaulted ceiling and a cozy fireplace
- Two bedrooms on the second floor share a bath
- 3 bedrooms, 2 1/2 baths, 2-car drive under garage
- Basement or crawl space foundation, please specify when ordering

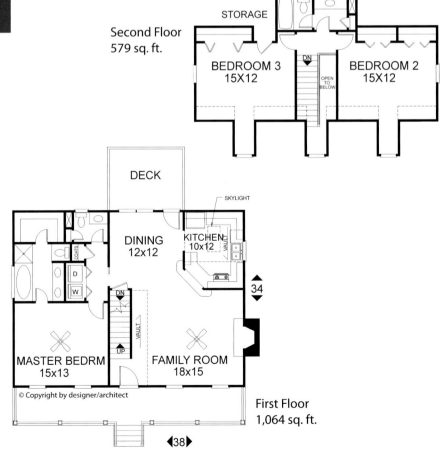

Second Floor
579 sq. ft.

STORAGE

BEDROOM 3
15X12

DN

OPEN
TO
BELOW

BEDROOM 2
15X12

DECK

SKYLIGHT

DINING
12x12

KITCHEN
10x12

VAULT

34

COATS

D

W

DN

VAULT

UP

MASTER BEDRM
15x13

FAMILY ROOM
18x15

© Copyright by designer/architect

First Floor
1,064 sq. ft.

◄38►

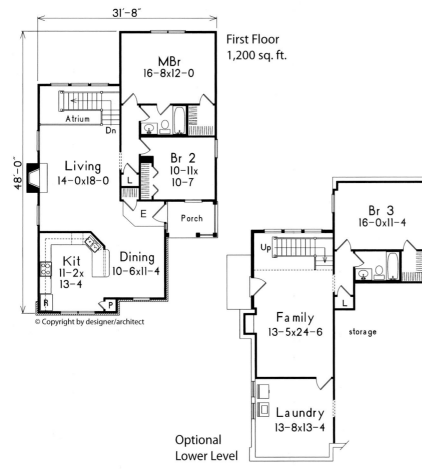

31'-8"

First Floor
1,200 sq. ft.

MBr
16-8x12-0

Atrium

Dn

Living
14-0x18-0

Br 2
10-11x
10-7

48'-0"

L

E

Porch

Kit
11-2x
13-4

Dining
10-6x11-4

R

P

© Copyright by designer/architect

Up

Br 3
16-0x11-4

Family
13-5x24-6

storage

L

Laundry
13-8x13-4

Optional
Lower Level

Special features

- 1,200 total square feet of living area
- Entry leads to a large dining area which opens to the kitchen and sun-drenched living room
- An expansive window wall in the two-story atrium lends space and light to living room with fireplace
- The large kitchen features a breakfast bar, built-in pantry and storage galore
- 697 square feet of optional living area on the lower level includes a family room, bedroom #3 and a bath
- 2 bedrooms, 1 bath
- Walk-out basement foundation

Rear Elevation

Special features

- 1,768 total square feet of living area
- Uniquely designed vaulted living and dining rooms combine making great use of space
- Informal family room has a vaulted ceiling, plant shelf accents and kitchen overlook
- Sunny breakfast area conveniently accesses the kitchen
- 3 bedrooms, 2 baths, 2-car garage
- Slab foundation

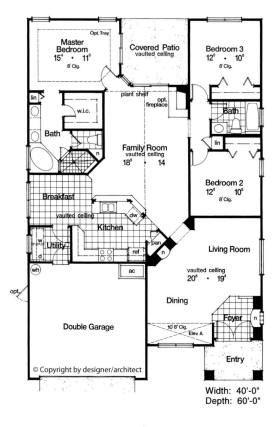

© Copyright by designer/architect

Width: 40'-0"
Depth: 60'-0"

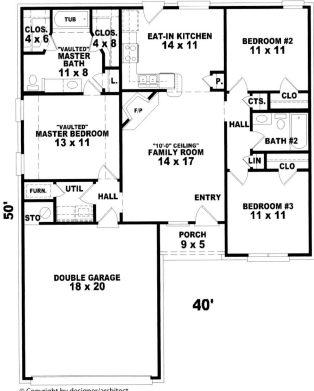

© Copyright by designer/architect

CLOS. 4 x 6

TUB

CLOS. 4 x 8

"VAULTED" **MASTER BATH** 11 x 8

EAT-IN KITCHEN 14 x 11

BEDROOM #2 11 x 11

L.

P.

F/P

CTS.

CLO

HALL

BATH #2

"VAULTED" **MASTER BEDROOM** 13 x 11

"10'-0" CEILING" **FAMILY ROOM** 14 x 17

LIN

CLO

FURN.

UTIL

HALL

ENTRY

BEDROOM #3 11 x 11

STO

PORCH 9 x 5

50'

DOUBLE GARAGE 18 x 20

40'

Special features

- 1,210 total square feet of living area
- The home enters to view the spacious family room that features a 10' ceiling and corner fireplace
- The eat-in kitchen has plenty of workspace and access to the rear patio
- The split-bedroom design ensures privacy with two secondary bedrooms sharing a full bath and the master bedroom featuring a deluxe bath and vaulted ceiling
- 3 bedrooms, 2 baths, 2-car garage
- Slab foundation

Special features

- 342 total square feet of living area
- Two-story structure is attractively disguised as a one-story
- The side entrance leads to an entry that accesses both the garage and the second floor studio
- A laundry room on the first floor doubles as a mud room between the garage and rear entry
- The second floor studio apartment includes a kitchenette area, full bath and closet
- Studio room, 1 bath, 1-car garage
- Slab foundation

Rear Elevation

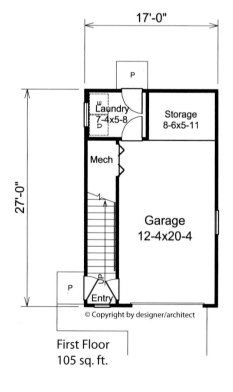

17'-0"

27'-0"

P

Laundry
7-4x5-8

Storage
8-6x5-11

Mech

Garage
12-4x20-4

P

Entry

© Copyright by designer/architect

First Floor
105 sq. ft.

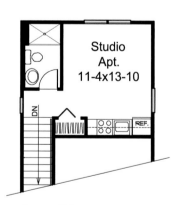

Studio
Apt.
11-4x13-10

DN

REF.

Second Floor
237 sq. ft.

Special features

- 1,053 total square feet of living area
- Energy efficient home with 2" x 6" exterior walls
- Spacious kitchen and dining room
- Roomy bath includes an oversized tub
- Entry has a handy coat closet
- 3 bedrooms, 1 bath
- Basement foundation

© Copyright by designer/architect

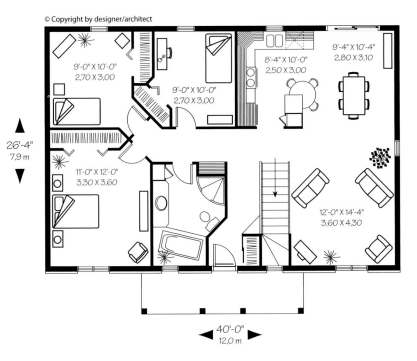

9'-0" X 10'-0"
2,70 X 3,00

9'-0" X 10'-0"
2,70 X 3,00

8'-4" X 10'-0"
2,50 X 3,00

9'-4" X 10'-4"
2,80 X 3,10

11'-0" X 12'-0"
3,30 X 3,60

12'-0" X 14'-4"
3,60 X 4,30

26'-4"
7,9 m

40'-0"
12,0 m

Special features

- 1,873 total square feet of living area
- Interesting contemporary roof lines
- Vaulted living room is separated from foyer by glass block wall
- Spacious sun room with skylights adjoins living room
- Kitchen has a useful breakfast bar
- Master bedroom has all the pleasing amenities including a balcony
- 3 bedrooms, 2 1/2 baths, 2-car garage
- Basement foundation, drawings also include slab and partial basement/crawl space foundations

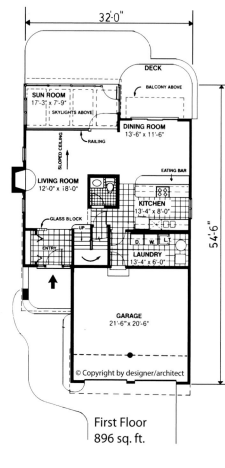

32'-0"

DECK

BALCONY ABOVE

SUN ROOM
17'-3" x 7'-9"
SKYLIGHTS ABOVE

DINING ROOM
13'-6" x 11'-6"

SLOPED CEILING

RAILING

EATING BAR

LIVING ROOM
12'-0" x 18'-0"

KITCHEN
13'-4" x 8'-0"

GLASS BLOCK

UP

ENTRY

D W

LAUNDRY
13'-4" x 6'-0"

54'-6"

GARAGE
21'-6" x 20'-6"

© Copyright by designer/architect

First Floor
896 sq. ft.

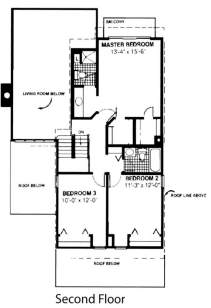

BALCONY

MASTER BEDROOM
13'-4" x 15'-6"

LIVING ROOM BELOW

DN

ROOF BELOW

BEDROOM 3
10'-0" x 12'-0"

BEDROOM 2
11'-3" x 12'-0"

ROOF LINE ABOVE

ROOF BELOW

Second Floor
977 sq. ft.

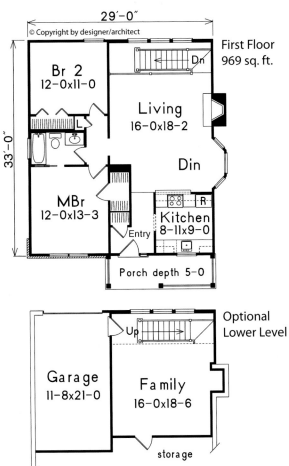

29'-0"

© Copyright by designer/architect

First Floor
969 sq. ft.

33'-0"

Br 2
12-0x11-0

Living
16-0x18-2

Dn

MBr
12-0x13-3

Din

Entry

Kitchen
8-11x9-0

R

L

Porch depth 5-0

Optional
Lower Level

Up

Garage
11-8x21-0

Family
16-0x18-6

storage

Special features

- 969 total square feet of living area
- Eye-pleasing facade enjoys stone accents with country porch for quiet evenings
- A bayed dining area, cozy fireplace and atrium with sunny two-story windows are the many features of the living room
- Step-saver kitchen includes a pass-through snack bar
- 325 square feet of optional living area on the lower level
- 2 bedrooms, 1 bath, 1-car drive under rear entry garage
- Walk-out basement foundation

Rear Elevation

Special features

- 1,400 total square feet of living area
- Energy efficient home with 2" x 6" exterior walls
- A wall of windows in the dining room is cheerful and brilliant
- Attic storage is a welcome addition to the second floor
- The master bedroom is enticing and elegant with a bay window, private bath and walk-in closet
- 3 bedrooms, 2 1/2 baths
- Crawl space foundation

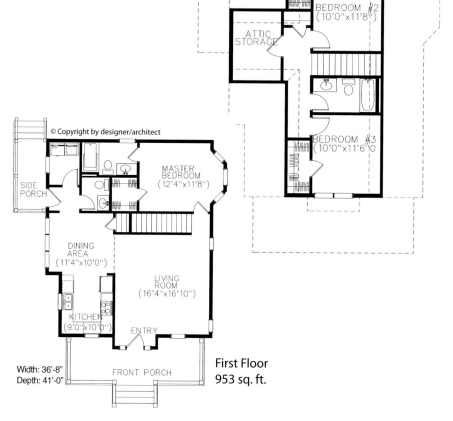

Second Floor
447 sq. ft.

ATTIC STORAGE

BEDROOM #2
(10'0"x11'8")

BEDROOM #3
(10'0"x11'6"0)

© Copyright by designer/architect

SIDE PORCH

MASTER BEDROOM
(12'4"x11'8")

DINING AREA
(11'4"x10'0")

LIVING ROOM
(16'4"x16'10")

KITCHEN
(9'0"x10'0")

ENTRY

Width: 36'-8"
Depth: 41'-0"

FRONT PORCH

First Floor
953 sq. ft.

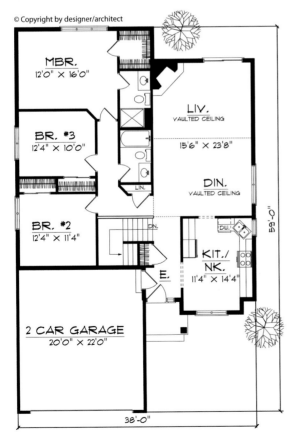

© Copyright by designer/architect

MBR.
12'0" × 16'0"

LIV.
VAULTED CEILING

15'6" × 23'8"

BR. #3
12'4" × 10'0"

DIN.
VAULTED CEILING

LIN.

BR. #2
12'4" × 11'4"

DN.

KIT./
NK.
11'4" × 14'4"

DW.

E.

2 CAR GARAGE
20'0" × 22'0"

59'-0"

38'-0"

Special features

- 1,448 total square feet of living area
- Energy efficient home with 2" x 6" exterior walls
- Corner fireplace warms the living and dining rooms
- The kitchen and nook combine for a spacious informal living area
- Bedrooms are located away from main living areas for privacy
- 3 bedrooms, 2 baths, 2-car garage
- Basement foundation

Special features

- 1,211 total square feet of living area
- Extraordinary views are enjoyed in the vaulted family room through sliding doors
- Functional kitchen features snack bar and laundry closet
- Bedroom and bunk room complete first floor while a large bedroom with two storage areas and balcony complete the second floor
- Additional plan for second floor creates 223 square feet of additional bedroom space
- 2 bedrooms, 1 bath
- Crawl space foundation, drawings also include basement foundation

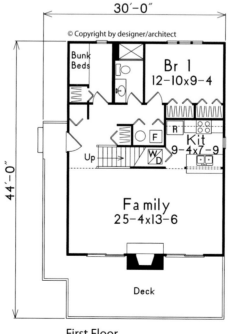

30'-0"

© Copyright by designer/architect

Bunk Beds

Br 1
12-10x9-4

44'-0"

Up

Kit
9-4x7-9

W
D

Family
25-4x13-6

Deck

First Floor
884 sq. ft.

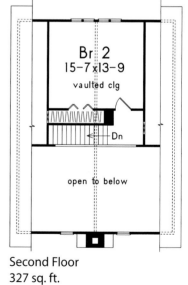

Br 2
15-7x13-9
vaulted clg

Dn

open to below

Second Floor
327 sq. ft.

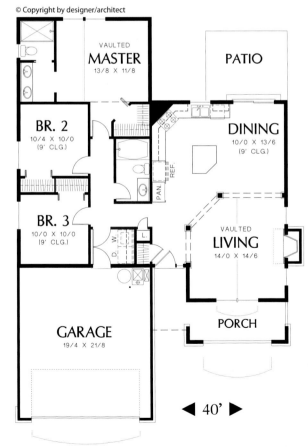

© Copyright by designer/architect

VAULTED
MASTER
13/8 X 11/8

PATIO

BR. 2
10/4 X 10/0
(9' CLG.)

DINING
10/0 X 13/6
(9' CLG.)

REF.

PAN.

BR. 3
10/0 X 10/0
(9' CLG.)

D. W.

VAULTED
LIVING
14/0 X 14/6

GARAGE
19/4 X 21/8

PORCH

58'

◀ 40' ▶

Special features

- 1,275 total square feet of living area
- Energy efficient home with 2" x 6" exterior walls
- The kitchen expands into the dining area with the help of a center island
- Decorative columns keep the living area open to other areas
- Covered front porch adds charm to the entry
- 3 bedrooms, 2 baths, 2-car garage
- Crawl space foundation

Special features

- 1,670 total square feet of living area
- Lots of closet space throughout
- Family room is flooded with sunlight from many windows
- Open living areas make this home appear larger
- 3 bedrooms, 2 1/2 baths, 2-car garage
- Basement foundation

First Floor
978 sq. ft.

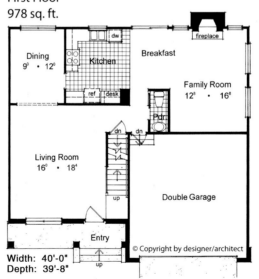

Dining
9⁰ • 12⁰

Kitchen

Breakfast

dw

fireplace

Family Room
12⁸ • 16⁸

ref desk

Pdr.

Living Room
16⁰ • 18⁴

dn   dn

up

Double Garage

Entry

up

Width: 40'-0"
Depth: 39'-8"

© Copyright by designer/architect

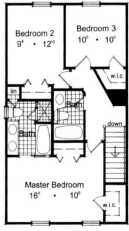

Bedroom 2
9⁴ • 12¹⁰

Bedroom 3
10⁰ • 10⁰

w.i.c.

lin

Bath

Bath

down

Master Bedroom
16⁰ • 10⁶

w.i.c.

Second Floor
692 sq. ft.

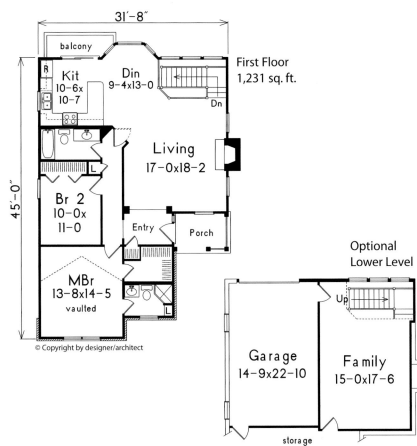

31'-8"

balcony

Kit
10-6x
10-7

Din
9-4x13-0

First Floor
1,231 sq. ft.

Dn

45'-0"

Living
17-0x18-2

Br 2
10-0x
11-0

Entry

Porch

MBr
13-8x14-5
vaulted

© Copyright by designer/architect

Optional
Lower Level

Up

Garage
14-9x22-10

Family
15-0x17-6

storage

Special features

- 1,231 total square feet of living area
- Dutch gables and stone accents provide an enchanting appearance
- The spacious living room offers a masonry fireplace, atrium with window wall and is open to a dining area with bay window
- Kitchen has a breakfast counter, lots of cabinet space and glass sliding doors to a balcony
- 380 square feet of optional living area on the lower level
- 2 bedrooms, 2 baths, 1-car drive under rear entry garage
- Walk-out basement foundation

Rear Elevation

Side View

Special features

- 1,133 total square feet of living area
- This home is designed to fit narrow lots with the main entry on the side
- A U-shaped kitchen includes a breakfast area and porch access
- Split bedrooms ensure privacy for the master bedroom suite
- 3 bedrooms, 2 baths, 1-car garage
- Slab foundation

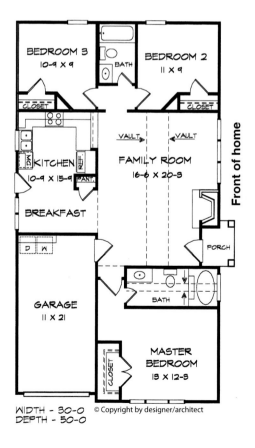

BEDROOM 3
10-9 X 9

BATH

BEDROOM 2
11 X 9

CLOSET

CLOSET

VAULT   VAULT

KITCHEN
10-9 X 15-9

FAMILY ROOM
16-6 X 20-3

Front of home

PANT.

BREAKFAST

PORCH

D   W

BATH

GARAGE
11 X 21

CLOSET

MASTER
BEDROOM
13 X 12-3

WIDTH - 30-0
DEPTH - 50-0

© Copyright by designer/architect

Special features

- 1,123 total square feet of living area
- Eating bar in kitchen extends dining area
- Dining area and great room flow together creating a sense of spaciousness
- Master suite has privacy from other bedrooms as well as a private bath
- Utility room is conveniently located near the kitchen
- 3 bedrooms, 2 baths
- Crawl space or slab foundation, please specify when ordering

© Copyright by designer/architect

MASTER SUITE
11'-0" X 13'-0"

BEDROOM-2
11'-0" X 9'-8"

F/P

MASTER BATH

CL.

FURN.

WASH DRY.

GREAT ROOM
14'-6" X 15'-1"

HALL

CL.

UTILITY

BATH-2

LIN.

REF.

FOYER

EATING BAR

CTS.

BEDROOM-3
11'-0" X 9'-0"

DINING
10'-0" X 10'-0"

D. W.

CL.

PORCH

S.   R.

KIT.

37'-6"

38'-0"

Special features

- 1,131 total square feet of living area
- Inviting porch and roof dormer create a charming exterior
- The spacious area on the first floor is perfect for a large shop, private studio, office or cottage great room and includes a fireplace, kitchenette and half bath
- Two bedrooms, a full bath and attic storage comprise the second floor which has its own private entrance and wide sunny hallway
- 2 bedrooms, 1 1/2 baths
- Slab foundation

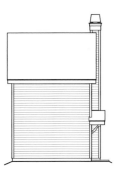

Rear Elevation

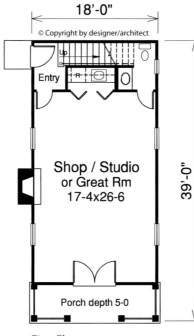

18'-0"

© Copyright by designer/architect

Entry

Shop / Studio
or Great Rm
17-4x26-6

39'-0"

Porch depth 5-0

First Floor
612 sq. ft.

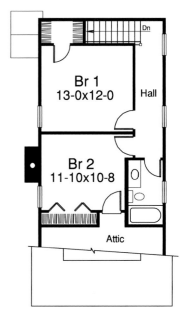

Dn

Br 1
13-0x12-0

Hall

Br 2
11-10x10-8

Attic

Second Floor
519 sq. ft.

First Floor
1,865 sq. ft.

Second Floor
753 sq. ft.

© Copyright by designer/architect

37'-0"

92'-8"

CARPORT
22'-8" X 21'-8"

STRG.

PATIO

COVERED
PORCH
16'-4" X 6'-4"

GREAT RM.
16'-0" X 26'-6"

BUILT
IN

MASTER BEDROOM
13'-8" X 16'-8"

BRKFAST
RM.
15'-0" X 9'-0"

LAU.

BUILT-IN

M. BATH
12'-2" X 15'-4"

GLASS
SHWR

SEA

LIN
M.C.

WHP
TUB

KITCHEN
16'-0" X 13'-0"

RG.

DW

REF.

LIVING RM.
11'-0" X 13'-8"

FOYER
9'-0" X 8'-0"

DINING RM.
11'-4" X 15'-8"

8" COLUMNS

PORCH

9' CEILING LINE

ATTIC STORAGE

BEDROOM 1
12'-6" X 14'-0"
9' CEILING LINE

LIN

LIN

SHLVS.

BEDROOM 2
12'-6" X 14'-0"
9' CEILING LINE

BATH

Special features

- 1,700 total square feet of living area
- Two-story entry with T-stair is illuminated with a decorative oval window
- Skillfully designed U-shaped kitchen has a built-in pantry
- All bedrooms have generous closet storage and are common to a spacious hall with a walk-in cedar closet
- 4 bedrooms, 2 1/2 baths, 2-car side entry garage
- Basement foundation

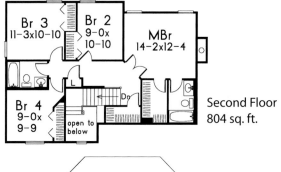

Br 3
11-3x10-10

Br 2
9-0x
10-10

MBr
14-2x12-4

Br 4
9-0x
9-9

open to below

Dn

Second Floor
804 sq. ft.

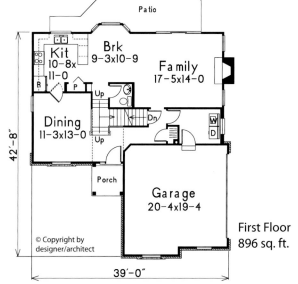

Patio

Kit
10-8x
11-0

Brk
9-3x10-9

Family
17-5x14-0

Dining
11-3x13-0

Up

Dn

Up

W
D

Porch

Garage
20-4x19-4

42'-8"

39'-0"

© Copyright by
designer/architect

First Floor
896 sq. ft.

Rear Elevation

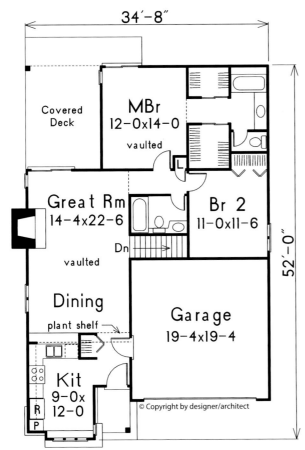

34'-8"

52'-0"

Covered Deck

MBr
12-0x14-0
vaulted

Great Rm
14-4x22-6

vaulted

Dn

Br 2
11-0x11-6

Dining

plant shelf

Garage
19-4x19-4

Kit
9-0x
12-0

© Copyright by designer/architect

Special features

■ 1,127 total square feet of living area
■ Plant shelf joins kitchen and dining room
■ Vaulted master bedroom has double walk-in closets, deck access and a private bath
■ Great room features a vaulted ceiling, fireplace and sliding doors to the covered deck
■ Ideal home for a narrow lot
■ 2 bedrooms, 2 baths, 2-car garage
■ Basement foundation

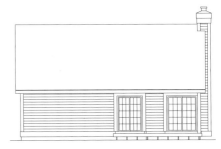

Rear Elevation

Special features

- 1,650 total square feet of living area
- The private master bedroom enjoys a whirlpool tub, walk-in closet and twin vanities
- The expansive great room is topped with a tray ceiling and also includes a built-in entertainment center and easy access to the kitchen and dining room
- A laundry room, walk-in hall closet and flex space offer the convenience every family needs
- 3 bedrooms, 2 baths, 2-car side entry garage
- Crawl space or slab foundation, please specify when ordering

© Copyright by designer/architect

Width: 35'-0"
Depth: 73'-4"

Two Car Garage
20-4 x 21-8

Storage

Master Bath
13-8 x 8-10
10-0 Ceiling

8' Ceiling
Jet Tub

Van.
Lin.

Shr.

Kitchen
12-6 x 14-6

Island

W D
Util.
6-8 x 6-4

Pan./ Cabs

Master Bedroom
14-6 x 13-4
10-0 Ceiling

Clos.
6-8 x 7-10

Clos.

Dining Room
12-6 x 12-4
10-0 Ceiling

Flex Space
6-8 x 7-8

Bedroom #2
11-6 x 11-0
10-0 Ceiling

Entertainment Center

Trayed Ceiling

Great Room
19-0 x 15-6
11-0 Ceiling

Hall

Hall Bath

Tub/ Shr.

Bedroom #3
11-6 x 11-0
10-0 Ceiling

Clos.

Covered Porch
35-0 x 8-0

Special features

- 1,332 total square feet of living area
- Home offers both basement and first floor entry locations
- A dramatic living room features a vaulted ceiling, fireplace, exterior balcony and dining area
- An L-shaped kitchen offers spacious cabinetry, breakfast area with bay window and access to the rear patio
- 3 bedrooms, 2 baths, 4-car tandem garage
- Walk-out basement foundation

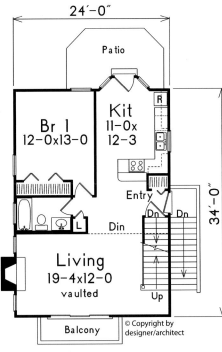

24´-0″

Patio

Kit
11-0x
12-3

Br 1
12-0x13-0

R

Entry

Dn   Dn

Din

Living
19-4x12-0
vaulted

Up

Balcony

34´-0″

© Copyright by designer/architect

First Floor
828 sq. ft.

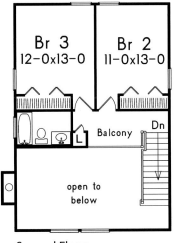

Br 3
12-0x13-0

Br 2
11-0x13-0

L

Balcony

Dn

open to below

Second Floor
504 sq. ft.

Rear Elevation

Special features

- 1,500 total square feet of living area
- Decorative columns adorn the entry into the formal dining room, keeping the area private yet maintaining an open feel
- The massive living room is the perfect space to relax or entertain guests with its close proximity to the kitchen
- Three bedrooms are located at the rear of the home, making this an ideal family design
- 3 bedrooms, 2 baths
- Crawl space foundation

MASTER BEDROOM
(11'0"x17'8")

BEDROOM #3
(10'4"x11'4")

BEDROOM #2
(10'0"x11'4")

KITCHEN
(11'0"x17'8")

LIVING ROOM
(21'4"x17'8")

DINING ROOM
(10'0"x11'4")

PORCH

W: 38'-0"
D: 58'-0"

Special features

- 733 total square feet of living area
- Bedrooms are separate from the kitchen and living area for privacy
- Lots of closet space throughout this home
- Centrally located bath is easily accessible
- Kitchen features a door accessing the outdoors and a door separating it from the rest of the home
- 2 bedrooms, 1 bath
- Pier foundation

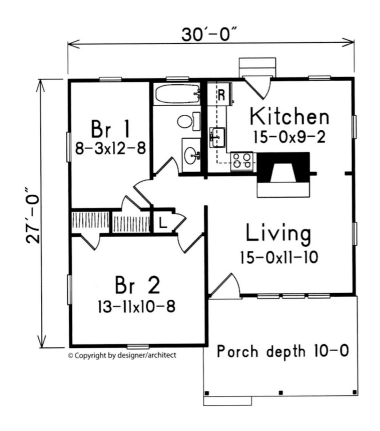

30'-0"

27'-0"

Br 1
8-3x12-8

Kitchen
15-0x9-2

Br 2
13-11x10-8

Living
15-0x11-10

Porch depth 10-0

© Copyright by designer/architect

Special features

- 902 total square feet of living area
- Vaulted entry with laundry room leads to a spacious second floor apartment
- The large living room features an entry coat closet, L-shaped kitchen with pantry and dining area/balcony overlooking atrium window wall
- Roomy bedroom with walk-in closet is convenient to hall bath
- 1 bedroom, 1 bath, 2-car side entry garage
- Slab foundation

Rear Elevation

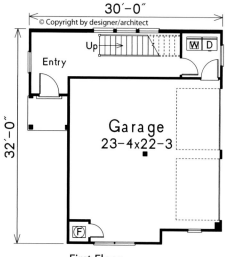

30'-0"

© Copyright by designer/architect

Up

W D

Entry

32'-0"

Garage
23-4x22-3

F

First Floor
238 sq. ft.

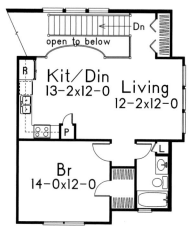

Dn

open to below

R

Kit/Din
13-2x12-0

Living
12-2x12-0

P

L

Br
14-0x12-0

Second Floor
664 sq. ft.

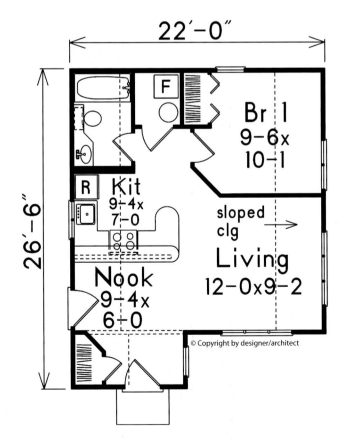

22'-0"

26'-6"

Br 1
9-6x
10-1

Kit
9-4x
7-0

sloped
clg →

Living
12-0x9-2

Nook
9-4x
6-0

F

R

© Copyright by designer/architect

Jackidyn
Damoco 07

Special features

- 527 total square feet of living area
- Cleverly arranged home has it all
- Foyer spills into the dining nook with access to side views
- An excellent kitchen offers a long breakfast bar and borders the living room with a free-standing fireplace
- A cozy bedroom has a full bath just across the hall
- 1 bedroom, 1 bath
- Crawl space foundation

Special features

- 1,536 total square feet of living area
- Energy efficient home with 2" x 6" exterior walls
- Sliding glass doors in the master bedroom lead to a terrific screened porch offering a quiet place to retreat
- Galley-style kitchen is compact yet convenient
- A sunny dining area extends off the kitchen
- 3 bedrooms, 2 1/2 baths
- Pier foundation

© Copyright by designer/architect

MASTER BEDROOM (16'4"x11'10")

SCREENED PORCH (10'2"x10'4")

LAUNDRY 8'2"x6'0"

KITCHEN (12'8"x8'0")

DINING AREA (9'10"x9'8")

LIVING ROOM (17'8"x14'2)

ENTRY 8'6"x4'10"

8' FRONT WRAP AROUND PORCH

Width: 36'-0"
Depth: 43'-8"

First Floor
1,038 sq. ft.

BEDROOM #2 (11'4"x9'10")

BATH

BEDROOM #3 (11'4"x9'10")

Second Floor
498 sq. ft.

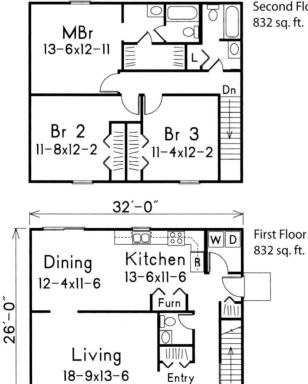

Second Floor
832 sq. ft.

MBr
13-6x12-11

L

Dn

Br 2
11-8x12-2

Br 3
11-4x12-2

32'-0"

26'-0"

First Floor
832 sq. ft.

Dining
12-4x11-6

Kitchen
13-6x11-6

W | D

R

Furn

Living
18-9x13-6

Entry

Up

© Copyright by designer/architect

Porch

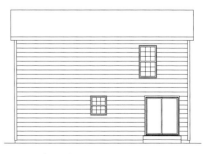

Rear Elevation

Special features

- 1,171 total square feet of living area
- This home is perfect for a starter home, second home on a lake or countryside setting
- The vaulted living room offers many exciting features including a corner fireplace and dining area with sliding doors to the side patio
- A built-in pantry, vaulted ceiling and breakfast bar are just a few amenities of the delightful kitchen
- 3 bedrooms, 2 baths, 2-car garage
- Basement foundation, drawings also include slab and crawl space foundations

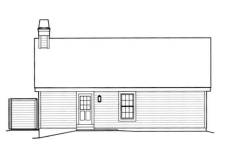

Rear Elevation

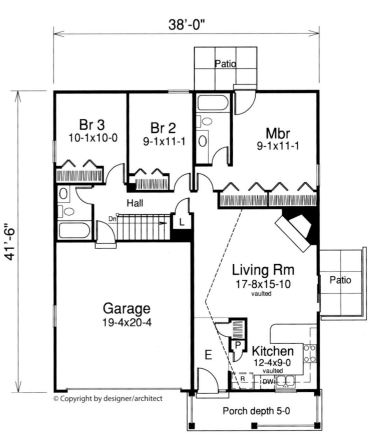

38'-0"

41'-6"

Patio

Br 3
10-1x10-0

Br 2
9-1x11-1

Mbr
9-1x11-1

Hall

Dn

L

Garage
19-4x20-4

Living Rm
17-8x15-10
vaulted

Patio

E

P

Kitchen
12-4x9-0
vaulted

R

DW

© Copyright by designer/architect

Porch depth 5-0

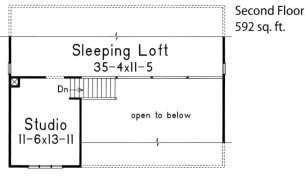

Second Floor
592 sq. ft.

Sleeping Loft
35-4x11-5

Dn

open to below

Studio
11-6x13-11

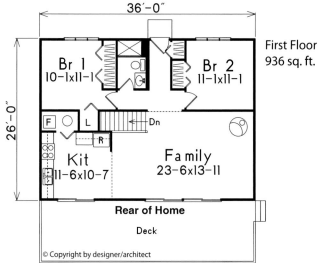

36'-0"

26'-0"

Br 1
10-1x11-1

Br 2
11-1x11-1

F L

R

Dn

Kit
11-6x10-7

Family
23-6x13-11

Rear of Home

Deck

First Floor
936 sq. ft.

Special features

- 1,528 total square feet of living area
- Large deck complements exterior
- Family room provides a welcome space for family get-togethers and includes a sloped ceiling and access to the studio and sleeping loft
- Kitchen features dining space and a view to the deck
- A hall bath is shared by two bedrooms on the first floor which have ample closet space
- 2 bedrooms, 1 bath
- Crawl space foundation

Rear View

Special features

- 1,224 total square feet of living area
- The coffered ceiling and corner fireplace provide an impressive entry view
- The adjoining kitchen includes an island with seating that opens to the cozy dining area
- The massive master bedroom features a vaulted ceiling and private bath with double-door entry and walk-in closet
- 3 bedrooms, 2 baths
- Slab foundation

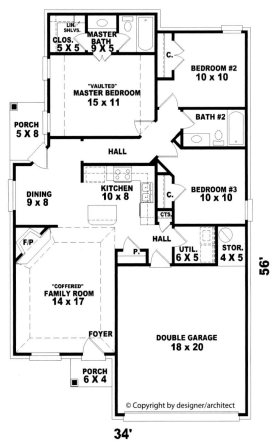

LIN. SHLVS.

MASTER BATH 9 X 5

CLOS. 5 X 5

C.

BEDROOM #2 10 x 10

"VAULTED" MASTER BEDROOM 15 x 11

BATH #2

PORCH 5 X 8

HALL

C.

BEDROOM #3 10 x 10

DINING 9 x 8

KITCHEN 10 x 8

CTS.

"COFFERED" FAMILY ROOM 14 x 17

F/P

HALL

P.

UTIL. 6 X 5

STOR. 4 X 5

FOYER

DOUBLE GARAGE 18 x 20

56'

PORCH 6 X 4

© Copyright by designer/architect

34'

Special features

- 1,120 total square feet of living area
- Master bedroom includes a half bath with laundry area, linen closet and kitchen access
- Kitchen has charming double-door entry, breakfast bar and a convenient walk-in pantry
- Welcoming front porch opens to a large living room with coat closet
- 3 bedrooms, 1 1/2 baths
- Crawl space foundation, drawings also include basement and slab foundations

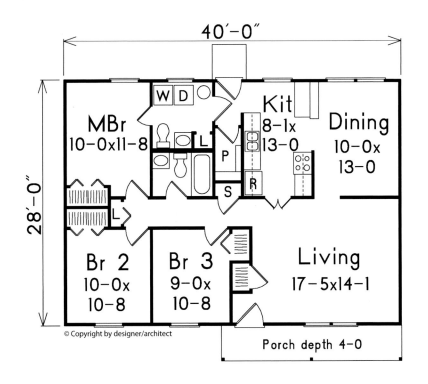

40'-0"

28'-0"

MBr
10-0x11-8

W D

Kit
8-1x
13-0

Dining
10-0x
13-0

L

P

S

R

Br 2
10-0x
10-8

Br 3
9-0x
10-8

Living
17-5x14-1

Porch depth 4-0

© Copyright by designer/architect

Rear Elevation

Special features

- 1,516 total square feet of living area
- Spacious great room is open to dining area with a bay and unique stair location
- Attractive and well-planned kitchen offers breakfast bar and built-in pantry
- Smartly designed master bedroom enjoys patio view
- 3 bedrooms, 2 baths, 2-car garage
- Basement foundation

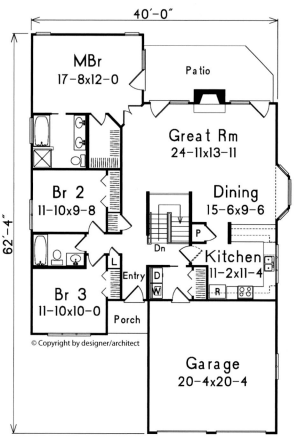

40'-0"

62'-4"

MBr
17-8x12-0

Patio

Great Rm
24-11x13-11

Br 2
11-10x9-8

Dining
15-6x9-6

Dn

P

Kitchen
11-2x11-4

L

Entry

D
W

R

Br 3
11-10x10-0

Porch

Garage
20-4x20-4

© Copyright by designer/architect

Rear Elevation

Special features

- 1,280 total square feet of living area
- Attention to architectural detail has created the look of an authentic Swiss cottage
- Spacious living room, adjacent kitchenette and dining area all enjoy views to the front deck
- Hall bath shared by two sizable bedrooms is included on the first and second floors
- 4 bedrooms, 2 baths
- Crawl space foundation, drawings also include basement foundation

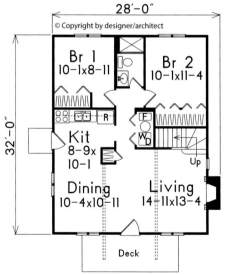

28'-0"

© Copyright by designer/architect

Br 1
10-1x8-11

Br 2
10-1x11-4

Kit
8-9x
10-1

R

F
W
D

Up

32'-0"

Dining
10-4x10-11

Living
14-11x13-4

Deck

First Floor
832 sq. ft.

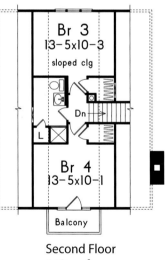

Br 3
13-5x10-3

sloped clg

Dn

L

Br 4
13-5x10-1

Balcony

Second Floor
448 sq. ft.

Special features

- 1,484 total square feet of living area
- Energy efficient home with 2" x 6" exterior walls
- Useful screened porch is ideal for dining and relaxing
- Corner fireplace warms the living room
- Snack bar adds extra counterspace in kitchen
- 3 bedrooms, 2 baths
- Basement foundation

First Floor
908 sq. ft.

Second Floor
576 sq. ft.

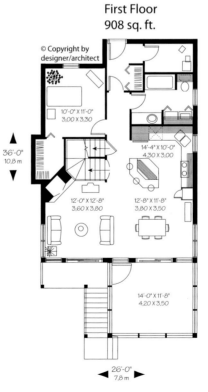

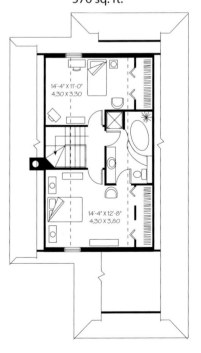

10'-0" X 11'-0"
3,00 X 3,30

14'-4" X 10'-0"
4,30 X 3,00

12'-0" X 12'-8"
3,60 X 3,80

12'-8" X 11'-8"
3,80 X 3,50

14'-0" X 11'-8"
4,20 X 3,50

36'-0"
10,8 m

26'-0"
7,8 m

14'-4" X 11'-0"
4,30 X 3,30

14'-4" X 12'-8"
4,30 X 3,80

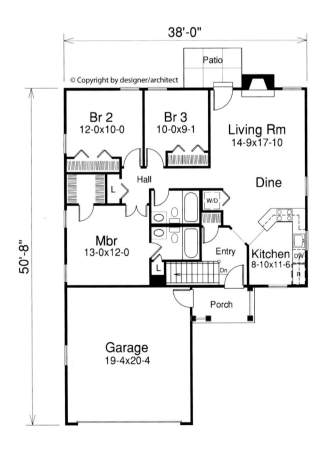

38'-0"

Patio

© Copyright by designer/architect

Br 2
12-0x10-0

Br 3
10-0x9-1

Living Rm
14-9x17-10

Hall

L

Dine

W/D

Mbr
13-0x12-0

Entry

Kitchen
8-10x11-6

L

Dn

DW

R

50'-8"

Porch

Garage
19-4x20-4

Special features

- 1,140 total square feet of living area
- Delightful appearance with a protective porch
- The entry, with convenient stairs to the basement, leads to spacious living and dining rooms open to the adjacent kitchen
- The master bedroom enjoys a double-door entry, walk-in closet and a private bath with its own linen closet
- 3 bedrooms, 2 baths, 2-car garage
- Basement foundation, drawings also include slab and crawl space foundations

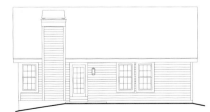

Rear Elevation

Special features

- 1,543 total square feet of living area
- Energy efficient home with 2" x 6" exterior walls
- The large country kitchen enjoys breezes entering the home through double-doors leading to a large deck
- The family room has a cheerful presence with windows on several walls, great for taking in the surrounding views
- Two second floor bedrooms skillfully share a full bath
- 4 bedrooms, 2 baths
- Pier foundation

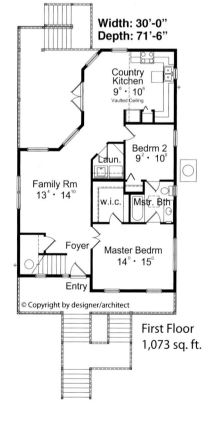

Width: 30'-0"
Depth: 71'-6"

Country Kitchen
$9^6 \cdot 10^6$
Vaulted Ceiling

Bedrm 2
$9^2 \cdot 10^0$

Laun.

Family Rm
$13^4 \cdot 14^{10}$

w.i.c.

Mstr. Bth

Foyer

Master Bedrm
$14^0 \cdot 15^0$

Entry

© Copyright by designer/architect

First Floor
1,073 sq. ft.

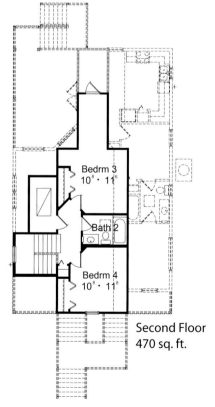

Bedrm 3
$10^8 \cdot 11^6$

Bath 2

Bedrm 4
$10^8 \cdot 11^8$

Second Floor
470 sq. ft.

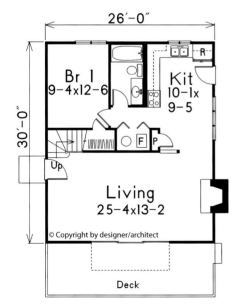

26'-0"

30'-0"

Br 1
9-4x12-6

Kit
10-1x
9-5

R

Up

F P

Living
25-4x13-2

© Copyright by designer/architect

Deck

First Floor
780 sq. ft.

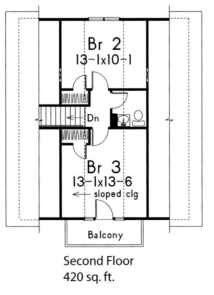

Br 2
13-1x10-1

Dn

Br 3
13-1x13-6
← sloped clg

Balcony

Second Floor
420 sq. ft.

Special features

- 1,200 total square feet of living area
- Ornate ranch-style railing enhances exterior while the stone fireplace provides a visual anchor
- Spectacular living room features an inviting fireplace and adjoins a charming kitchen with dining area
- Two second floor bedrooms share a full bath
- 3 bedrooms, 1 1/2 baths
- Crawl space foundation, drawings also include slab foundation

Special features

- 647 total square feet of living area
- Large vaulted room for living/ sleeping has plant shelves on each end, stone fireplace and wide glass doors for views
- Roomy kitchen is vaulted and has a bayed dining area and fireplace
- Step down into a sunken and vaulted bath featuring a 6'-0" whirlpool tub-in-a-bay with shelves at each end for storage
- A large palladian window adorns each end of the cottage giving a cheery atmosphere throughout
- 1 living/sleeping room, 1 bath
- Crawl space foundation

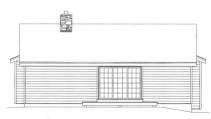

Rear Elevation

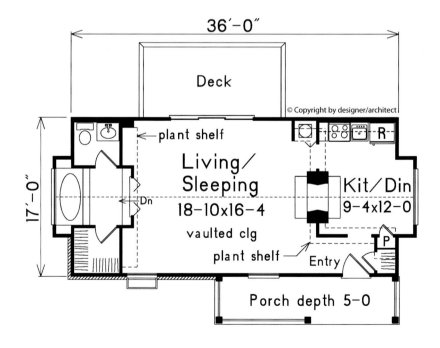

36'-0"

Deck

© Copyright by designer/architect

plant shelf

17'-0"

Living/ Sleeping
18-10x16-4

vaulted clg

plant shelf

Kit/Din
9-4x12-0

Dn

P

Entry

Porch depth 5-0

Special features

- 1,299 total square feet of living area
- Convenient storage for skis, etc. is located outside the front entrance
- The kitchen and dining room receive light from the box-bay window
- Large vaulted living room features a cozy fireplace and overlook from the second floor balcony
- Two second floor bedrooms share a Jack and Jill bath
- Second floor balcony extends over the entire length of the living room below
- 3 bedrooms, 2 baths
- Crawl space foundation, drawings also include slab foundation

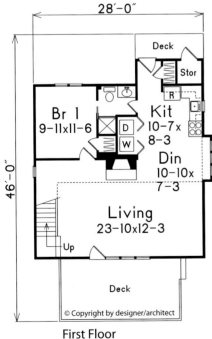

28'-0"

46'-0"

Deck

Stor

Br 1
9-11x11-6

Kit
10-7 x
8-3

R

Din
10-10x
7-3

Living
23-10x12-3

Up

Deck

© Copyright by designer/architect

First Floor
811 sq. ft.

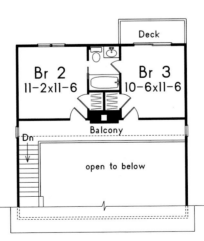

Deck

Br 2
11-2x11-6

Br 3
10-6x11-6

Balcony

Dn

open to below

Second Floor
488 sq. ft.

Special features

- 1,544 total square feet of living area
- Great room has a vaulted ceiling and fireplace
- 32' x 8' grilling porch in rear also features a supply room and cleaning table with sink
- Kitchen features a center island
- 3 bedrooms, 2 baths
- Crawl space or slab foundation, please specify when ordering

First Floor
1,031 sq. ft.

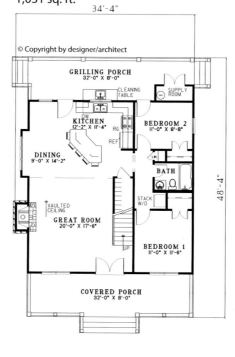

© Copyright by designer/architect

34'-4"

GRILLING PORCH
32'-0" X 8'-0"

CLEANING TABLE

SUPPLY ROOM

KITCHEN
12'-2" X 11'-4"

DW

RG.

REF

BEDROOM 2
11'-0" X 8'-8"

DINING
9'-0" X 14'-2"

LN

VAULTED CEILING

GREAT ROOM
20'-0" X 17'-8"

BATH

STACK W/D

UP

BEDROOM 1
11'-0" X 11'-6"

48'-4"

COVERED PORCH
32'-0" X 8'-0"

Second Floor
513 sq. ft.

SLOPED CEILING

STRG.

6' WALL

BATH

STRG.

8' REF. LINE

LOFT
20'-0" X 9'-0"

LN

DN

VAULTED CEILING

BEDROOM 3
11'-0" X 19'-6"

Special features

- 656 total square feet of living area
- Simple but cleverly designed exterior disguises this two-story structure as a one-story
- Located behind the garage is the perfect room for an office or workshop
- The front entrance leads to an entry that accesses both the garage and apartment
- A well-equipped kitchenette, full bath and a closet/mechanical room are the featured spaces of the efficient studio apartment
- Studio room, 1 bath, 1-car garage
- Slab foundation

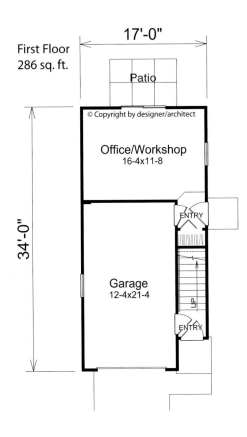

First Floor
286 sq. ft.

17'-0"

Patio

© Copyright by designer/architect

Office/Workshop
16-4x11-8

ENTRY

34'-0"

Garage
12-4x21-4

UP

ENTRY

Second Floor
370 sq. ft.

REF.

DW

Kit/Liv. Rm.
16-4x11-8

DN

F/
WH

Rear Elevation

Special features

- 1,872 total square feet of living area
- Kitchen has counter for dining that overlooks into great room
- Dining area directly accesses covered porch
- The upper porch connects to the master suite creating a quiet outdoor escape
- 3 bedrooms, 3 baths, 2-car rear entry garage
- Crawl space or slab foundation, please specify when ordering

First Floor
1,062 sq. ft.

Second Floor
804 sq. ft.

Second Floor
868 sq. ft.

walk-in clo.

BATH

BATH

BEDROOM
12'-8" x 12'-4"

c

dn.

MASTER
BEDROOM
13' x 15'

c

BEDROOM
15' x 11'-6"

roof

36'-0"

© Copyright by
designer/architect

30'-0"

6'-0"

FAMILY ROOM
16' x 13'-4"

beam ceiling

mud
room

d.

w.

KITCHEN
11' x 12'

C

B

dn.

walk-in
clo.

C

opt. opening

up

LIVING ROOM
13'-2" x 15'-8"

DINING OR
BEDROOM
15' x 12'

PORCH

First Floor
1,080 sq. ft.

Special features

- 1,948 total square feet of living area
- Family room offers warmth with an oversized fireplace and rustic beamed ceiling
- Fully-appointed kitchen extends into the family room
- Practical mud room is adjacent to the kitchen
- 3 bedrooms, 2 1/2 baths
- Basement foundation, drawings also include crawl space foundation

Special features

- 1,100 total square feet of living area
- The two bedrooms are larger than you would expect for a house of this size, and one includes a private bath with a whirlpool tub
- A separate laundry room, pantry, linen and hall closet add convenient storage and workspace to this design
- Relax with friends and family on either the front or rear covered porches
- 2 bedrooms, 2 baths
- Slab foundation

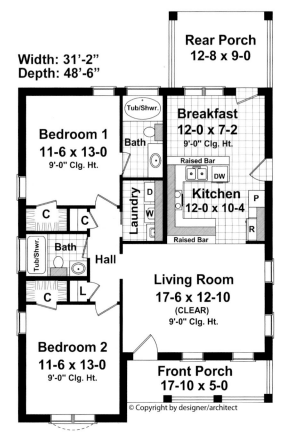

Width: 31'-2"
Depth: 48'-6"

Rear Porch
12-8 x 9-0

Bedroom 1
11-6 x 13-0
9'-0" Clg. Ht.

Tub/Shwr.

Bath

Breakfast
12-0 x 7-2
9'-0" Clg. Ht.

Raised Bar

DW

Kitchen
12-0 x 10-4

P

R

Raised Bar

C   C

Laundry

D

W

Tub/Shwr.

Bath

Hall

C   L

Living Room
17-6 x 12-10
(CLEAR)
9'-0" Clg. Ht.

Bedroom 2
11-6 x 13-0
9'-0" Clg. Ht.

Front Porch
17-10 x 5-0

© Copyright by designer/architect

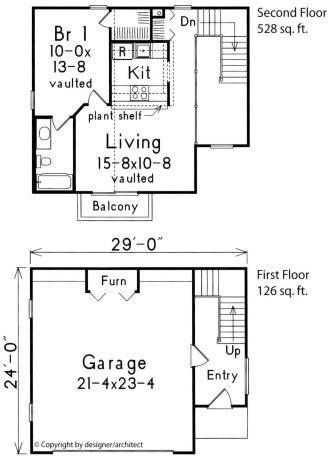

Second Floor
528 sq. ft.

Br 1
10-0x
13-8
vaulted

R

Kit

plant shelf

Dn

Living
15-8x10-8
vaulted

Balcony

29'-0"

24'-0"

Furn

Garage
21-4x23-4

Up

Entry

First Floor
126 sq. ft.

© Copyright by designer/architect

Special features

- 654 total square feet of living area
- Two-story vaulted entry has a balcony overlook and large windows to welcome the sun
- Vaulted living room is open to a pass-through kitchen and breakfast bar with an overhead plant shelf and features sliding glass doors to an outdoor balcony
- The bedroom with vaulted ceiling offers a private bath and walk-in closet
- 1 bedroom, 1 bath, 2-car garage
- Slab foundation

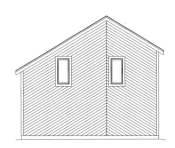

Rear Elevation

Special features

- 1,120 total square feet of living area
- Open living is created with the great room and dining room combining
- Private bath in the master suite
- Grilling porch in the rear of the home
- 2 bedrooms, 2 baths, 2-car rear entry garage
- Crawl space or slab foundation, please specify when ordering

28'-0"

GARAGE
19'-0" X 21'-0"

GRILLING
PORCH
8'-0" X 8'-0"

LAU.
7'-0" X 6'-0"

BEDROOM 2
12'-6" X 12'-0"

KITCHEN
9'-10" X 10'-2"

BATH
6'-0" X
9'-10"

BATH
6'-0" X
10'-10"

DINING
ROOM
14'-2" X 9'-6"

GREAT ROOM
14'-2" X 13'-0"

MASTER
SUITE
12'-6" X 13'-0"

69'-9"

COVERED PORCH
28'-0" X 8'-0"

26'-4"

Deck

DN

Living Room
14-0x12-8
Vaulted

First Floor
413 sq. ft.

Kitchen
12-0x7-10
Vaulted

28'-0"

DW. REF.

Entry

Garage
21-4x12-0

© Copyright by designer/architect

Patio

Mech.

Lower Level
358 sq. ft.

Bedroom
13-4x14-6

UP

Special features

- 771 total square feet of living area
- The living room includes a vaulted ceiling, separate entry with guest closet and glass doors to the rear deck
- A vaulted ceiling and overhead plant shelf are two attractive features of the L-shaped kitchen
- The lower level is comprised of a spacious bedroom complete with a private bath, walk-in closet and glass doors to the rear patio
- 1 bedroom, 1 1/2 baths, 1-car side entry garage
- Walk-out basement foundation

Rear Elevation

Special features

- 1,800 total square feet of living area
- The open kitchen flows nicely into the bayed dining room for a spacious, cheerful setting
- Enjoy outdoor meals on the rear covered porch that comes equipped with an outdoor kitchen
- An oversized laundry room and unique flex space add extra storage area for the growing family
- 3 bedrooms, 2 baths, 2-car side entry garage
- Slab or crawl space foundation, please specify when ordering

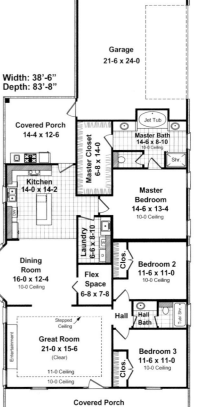

© Copyright by designer/architect

Width: 38'-6"
Depth: 83'-8"

Garage
21-6 x 24-0

Covered Porch
14-4 x 12-6

Master Closet
6-8 x 14-0

Jet Tub

Master Bath
14-6 x 8-10
10-0 Ceiling

Shr.

Kitchen
14-0 x 14-2

Master Bedroom
14-6 x 13-4
10-0 Ceiling

Laundry
6-6 x 8-10

Dining Room
16-0 x 12-4
10-0 Ceiling

Flex Space
6-8 x 7-8

Clos.

Bedroom 2
11-6 x 11-0
10-0 Ceiling

Stepped Ceiling

Hall

Hall Bath

Tub/ Shr

Entertainment

Great Room
21-0 x 15-6
(Clear)
11-0 Ceiling
10-0 Ceiling

Clos.

Bedroom 3
11-6 x 11-0
10-0 Ceiling

Covered Porch
36-6 x 8-0

Special features

- 1,492 total square feet of living area
- Cleverly angled entry spills into the living and dining rooms which share warmth from the fireplace flanked by arched windows
- Master bedroom includes a double-door entry, huge walk-in closet, shower and bath with picture window
- Stucco and dutch-hipped roofs add warmth and charm to facade
- 3 bedrooms, 2 1/2 baths, 2-car garage
- Basement foundation

35'-0"

Deck

Brk
9-0x
11-0

Kit

Dining
12-0x9-4

10-9x14-6

Dn

Living
15-8x14-0

P

L

Up

Porch

© Copyright by
designer/architect

41'-8"

Garage
19-4x21-4

First Floor
760 sq. ft.

MBr
11-0x14-8

Br 2
12-0x11-0

Dn

L

Br 3
12-0x9-9

raised
ceiling

Second Floor
732 sq. ft.

Rear Elevation

Special features

- 1,493 total square feet of living area
- First floor master bedroom maintains privacy
- Dining and great rooms have a feeling of spaciousness with two-story high ceilings
- Utilities are conveniently located near the garage entrance
- 3 bedrooms, 2 1/2 baths, 2-car garage
- Basement foundation

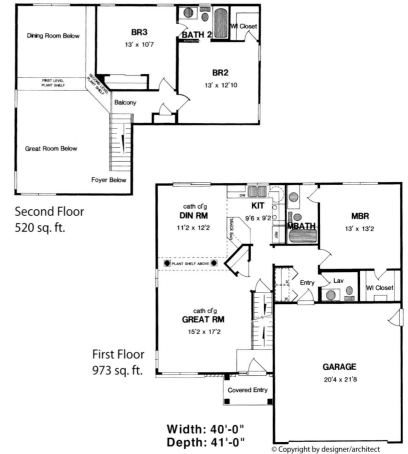

Second Floor
520 sq. ft.

Dining Room Below

BR3
13' x 10'7

BATH 2

WI Closet

BR2
13' x 12'10

FIRST LEVEL
PLANT SHELF

SECOND LEVEL
PLANT SHELF

Balcony

Great Room Below

Foyer Below

First Floor
973 sq. ft.

cath cl'g
DIN RM
11'2 x 12'2

KIT
9'6 x 9'2

MBR
13' x 13'2

MBATH

PLANT SHELF ABOVE

cath cl'g
GREAT RM
15'2 x 17'2

Entry

Lav

WI Closet

GARAGE
20'4 x 21'8

Covered Entry

Width: 40'-0"
Depth: 41'-0"

Special features

- 1,662 total square feet of living area
- Activity area becomes an ideal place for family gatherings
- Well-organized kitchen includes lots of storage space, a walk-in pantry and plenty of cabinetry
- The rear of the home features a versatile back porch for dining or relaxing
- Master bedroom has a bay window and private balcony
- 2 bedrooms, 1 1/2 baths
- Basement foundation

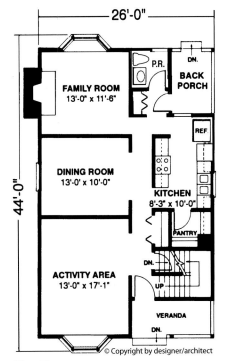

26'-0"

44'-0"

FAMILY ROOM
13'-0" x 11'-6"

P.R.

DN.

BACK PORCH

REF.

DINING ROOM
13'-0" x 10'-0"

KITCHEN
8'-3" x 10'-0"

PANTRY

DN.

UP

ACTIVITY AREA
13'-0" x 17'-1"

VERANDA

DN.

© Copyright by designer/architect

First Floor
1,092 sq. ft.

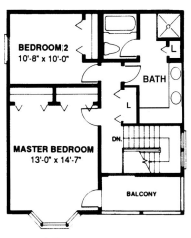

BEDROOM 2
10'-8" x 10'-0"

L

BATH

L

DN.

MASTER BEDROOM
13'-0" x 14'-7"

BALCONY

Second Floor
570 sq. ft.

Special features

- 1,294 total square feet of living area
- Great room features a fireplace and large bay with windows and patio doors
- Enjoy a laundry room immersed in light with large windows, an arched transom and attractive planter box
- Vaulted master bedroom features a bay window and two walk-in closets
- Bedroom #2 boasts a vaulted ceiling, plant shelf and half bath, perfect for a studio
- 2 bedrooms, 1 full bath, 2 half baths, 1-car rear entry garage
- Basement foundation

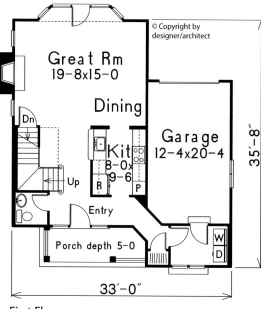

© Copyright by designer/architect

Great Rm
19-8x15-0

Dining

Kit
8-0x
9-6

Garage
12-4x20-4

Dn

Up

Entry

Porch depth 5-0

W
D

35'-8"

33'-0"

First Floor
718 sq. ft.

plant shelf

MBr
16-2x11-6
vaulted

Dn

Studio/
Br 2
12-10x12-1

plant shelf

vaulted

Second Floor
576 sq. ft.

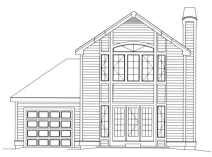

Rear Elevation

Special features

- 960 total square feet of living area
- Attractive appearance adds to any neighborhood
- A nice-sized living room leads to an informal family area with eat-in L-shaped kitchen, access to rear yard and basement space
- Three bedrooms with lots of closet space and a convenient hall bath complete the home
- 3 bedrooms, 1 bath
- Basement foundation, drawings also include crawl space and slab foundations

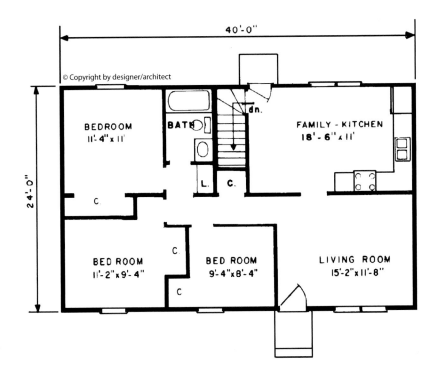

40'-0"

24'-0"

© Copyright by designer/architect

BEDROOM
11'-4" x 11'

BATH

FAMILY - KITCHEN
18'-6" x 11'

dn.

L. C.

C

BED ROOM
11'-2" x 9'-4"

C

BED ROOM
9'-4" x 8'-4"

C

LIVING ROOM
15'-2" x 11'-8"

Special features

- 1,587 total square feet of living area
- The large front porch opens to the spacious great room
- The kitchen is conveniently split around a center island for maximum use of space
- The master bedroom features a large walk-in closet and private bath with double-bowl vanity
- Daily traffic moves easily through the great room, kitchen and dining area
- 3 bedrooms, 2 baths
- Slab or crawl space foundation, please specify when ordering

CLO

LAUNDRY

MASTER BEDROOM
15'-0" X 14'-0"

LINEN

DINING AREA
13'-6" X 8'-2"

BEDROOM NO. 2
11'-0" X14'-0"

BATH 2

BATH 1

STOVE

KITCHEN
13'-6" X 12'-6"

REF

CLO

HVAC

HALL

GREAT ROOM
19'-0" X 18'-0"

LINEN

BEDROOM NO. 3
12'-0" X 14'-0"

CLO

PORCH

Width: 34'-0"
Depth: 52'-8"

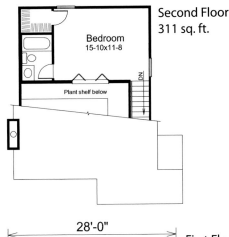

Second Floor
311 sq. ft.

Bedroom
15-10x11-8

Plant shelf below

DN

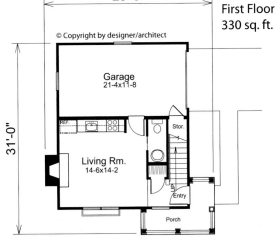

28'-0"

First Floor
330 sq. ft.

© Copyright by designer/architect

31'-0"

Garage
21-4x11-8

REF.

Stor.

Living Rm.
14-6x14-2

UP
Entry

Porch

- 641 total square feet of living area
- Charming exterior enjoys a wrap-around porch and a large feature window with arch and planter box
- The living room features a kitchenette, fireplace, vaulted ceiling with plant shelf, separate entry with coat closet and access to adjacent powder room and garage
- The stair leads to a spacious second floor bedroom complete with bath, walk-in closet and a unique opening with louvered doors for an overview of the living room below
- 1 bedroom, 1 1/2 baths, 1-car side entry garage
- Slab foundation

Rear Elevation

Special features

- 1,000 total square feet of living area
- Large mud room has a separate covered porch entrance
- Full-length covered front porch
- Bedrooms are on opposite sides of the home for privacy
- Vaulted ceiling creates an open and spacious feeling
- 2" x 6" exterior walls available, please order plan #598-058D-0085
- 2 bedrooms, 1 bath
- Crawl space foundation

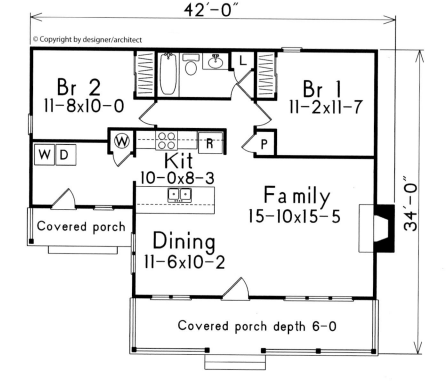

© Copyright by designer/architect

42'-0"

34'-0"

Br 2
11-8x10-0

Br 1
11-2x11-7

W D

Kit
10-0x8-3

P

Covered porch

Family
15-10x15-5

Dining
11-6x10-2

Covered porch depth 6-0

Quality plans for building your future, with extras that provide unsurpassed value, ensure good construction and long-term enjoyment.

A quality home - one that looks good, functions well, and provides years of enjoyment - is a product of many things - design, materials, craftsmanship.

But it's also the result of outstanding blueprints - the actual plans and specifications that tell the builder exactly how to build your home.

And with our *BLUEPRINT PACKAGES* you get the absolute best. A complete set of blueprints is available for every design in this book. These "working drawings" are highly detailed, resulting in two key benefits:

- **Better understanding by the contractor of how to build your home and...**

- **More accurate construction estimates.**

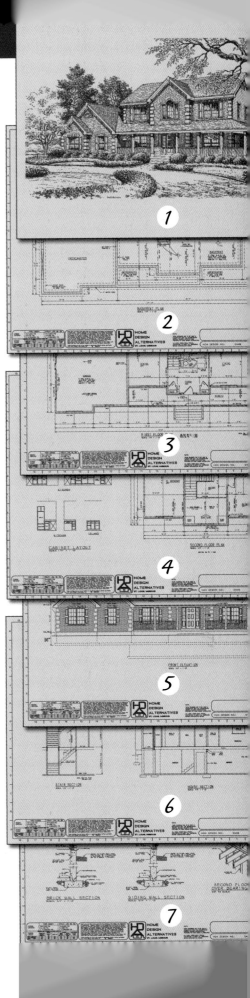

1. Cover Sheet is the artist's rendering of the exterior of the home and is included with many of the plans. It will give you an idea of how your home will look when completed and landscaped.

2. Foundation Plan shows the layout of the basement, crawl space, slab or pier foundation. All necessary notations and dimensions are included. See the plan page for the foundation types included. If the home plan you choose does not have your desired foundation type, our Customer Service Representatives can advise you on how to customize your foundation to suit your specific needs or site conditions.

3. Floor Plans show the placement of walls, doors, closets, plumbing fixtures, electrical outlets, columns, and beams for each level of the home.

4. Interior Elevations provide views of special interior elements such as fireplaces, kitchen cabinets, built-in units and other features of the home.

5. Exterior Elevations illustrate the front, rear and both sides of the house, with all details of exterior materials and the required dimensions.

6. Sections show detail views of the home or portions of the home as if it were sliced from the roof to the foundation. This sheet shows important areas such as load-bearing walls, stairs, joists, trusses and other structural elements, which are critical for proper construction.

7. Details show how to construct certain components of your home, such as the roof system, stairs, deck, etc.

Plan Number	Square Feet	Price Code	Page	Material List	Right Read. Reverse	Can. Shipping
598-001D-0033	1,624	B	85	•		
598-001D-0035	1,396	A	95	•		
598-001D-0036	1,320	A	41	•		
598-001D-0039	864	AAA	103	•		
598-001D-0040	864	AAA	37	•		
598-001D-0041	1,000	AA	44	•		
598-001D-0055	1,705	B	107	•		
598-001D-0056	1,705	B	152	•		
598-001D-0059	2,050	C	66	•		
598-001D-0060	1,818	C	158	•		
598-001D-0085	720	AAA	57	•		
598-001D-0086	1,154	AA	48	•		
598-001D-0087	1,230	A	63	•		
598-001D-0088	800	AAA	51	•		
598-001D-0089	1,000	AA	184	•		
598-001D-0092	1,664	B	221	•		
598-001D-0093	1,120	AA	225	•		
598-007D-0013	1,492	A	243	•		
598-007D-0014	1,985	C	50	•		
598-007D-0027	654	AAA	239	•		
598-007D-0028	1,711	B	55	•		
598-007D-0029	576	AAA	192	•		
598-007D-0031	1,092	AA	67	•		
598-007D-0032	1,294	A	246	•		
598-007D-0038	1,524	B	141	•		
598-007D-0040	632	AAA	78	•		
598-007D-0041	1,700	B	212	•		
598-007D-0042	914	AA	43	•		
598-007D-0043	647	AAA	232	•		
598-007D-0044	1,516	B	226	•		
598-007D-0054	1,575	B	35	•		
598-007D-0060	1,268	B	6	•		
598-007D-0061	1,340	A	71	•		
598-007D-0070	929	AA	74	•		
598-007D-0073	902	AA	218	•		
598-007D-0087	1,332	A	215	•		
598-007D-0088	1,299	A	178	•		
598-007D-0102	1,452	A	46	•		
598-007D-0103	1,231	A	207	•		
598-007D-0104	969	AA	201	•		
598-007D-0105	1,084	AA	62	•		
598-007D-0106	1,200	A	195	•		
598-007D-0107	1,161	AA	38	•		
598-007D-0108	983	AA	185	•		
598-007D-0109	888	AAA	159	•		
598-007D-0110	1,169	AA	59	•		
598-007D-0111	1,498	A	134	•		
598-007D-0114	1,671	B	147	•		
598-007D-0122	2,054	C	130			
598-007D-0127	2,158	C	112			
598-007D-0130	2,046	C	127			
598-007D-0131	2,050	C	123			
598-007D-0133	1,316	A	117			
598-007D-0138	2,167	C	104			
598-007D-0142	480	AAA	83			
598-007D-0145	1,005	AA	93			
598-007D-0148	1,167	AA	101			
598-007D-0156	809	AAA	96			
598-007D-0159	615	AAA	163			
598-007D-0175	882	AAA	171			
598-007D-0176	1,202	A	175			
598-007D-0177	1,102	AA	189			
598-007D-0178	1,203	A	138			
598-007D-0179	1,131	AA	210			
598-007D-0180	1,171	AA	222			
598-007D-0181	1,140	AA	229			
598-007D-0188	656	AAA	235			
598-007D-0189	713	AAA	150			
598-007D-0191	641	AAA	249			
598-007D-0193	771	AAA	241			
598-007D-0195	342	AAA	198			
598-007D-0196	421	AAA	53			
598-008D-0016	768	AAA	60	•		
598-008D-0048	1,948	C	237	•		
598-008D-0065	1,873	C	200	•		
598-008D-0072	1,200	A	136	•		
598-008D-0074	1,662	B	245	•		
598-008D-0076	1,922	C	39	•		
598-008D-0121	960	AA	247	•		
598-008D-0135	1,836	C	64	•		
598-008D-0138	1,280	A	227	•		
598-008D-0141	1,211	A	204	•		
598-008D-0143	1,299	A	233	•		
598-008D-0152	1,260	A	142	•		
598-008D-0154	527	AAA	219	•		
598-008D-0155	1,200	A	231	•		
598-008D-0156	1,528	B	223	•		
598-008D-0159	733	AAA	217	•		
598-008D-0163	1,280	A	148	•		
598-008D-0176	986	AA	174	•		
598-010D-0004	1,617	B	161	•		
598-011D-0001	1,275	C	205		•	
598-011D-0016	1,902	D	168		•	
598-011D-0017	1,805	D	193		•	
598-011D-0018	1,500	C	183		•	
598-011D-0019	1,978	E	128		•	
598-011D-0020	2,304	D	153		•	
598-011D-0021	1,464	C	65		•	
598-011D-0022	1,994	D	145		•	
598-011D-0026	2,320	E	34		•	
598-011D-0037	2,262	E	135		•	
598-011D-0044	2,420	E	125		•	
598-013D-0001	1,050	AA	61	•		
598-013D-0011	1,643	B	194	•		
598-013D-0012	1,647	B	121	•		
598-013D-0013	1,621	C	115	•		
598-013D-0149	2,058	D	166	•		
598-015D-0021	1,584	B	94			
598-015D-0023	1,649	B	68	•		
598-016D-0013	1,352	A	82	•		
598-016D-0029	1,635	C	8	•		
598-016D-0055	1,040	B	91	•		
598-020D-0030	1,168	B	99	•		
598-021D-0008	1,266	A	86	•		
598-022D-0002	1,246	A	42	•		
598-022D-0006	1,443	A	165	•		
598-022D-0007	1,516	B	19	•		
598-022D-0014	1,556	B	28	•		
598-022D-0017	1,448	A	169	•		
598-022D-0020	988	AA	173	•		
598-022D-0021	1,020	AA	126	•		
598-022D-0022	1,270	A	176	•		
598-022D-0024	1,127	AA	213	•		
598-024D-0006	1,618	C	15	•		
598-024D-0020	2,356	E	31	•		
598-024D-0041	1,401	C	180	•		
598-024D-0043	1,768	C	22	•		
598-025D-0001	1,123	AA	209	•		
598-025D-0036	2,565	D	170	•		
598-025D-0043	2,613	E	190	•		
598-026D-0161	1,375	A	30	•	•	
598-026D-0162	1,575	B	27	•		
598-026D-0220	1,699	H	36	•		
598-026D-0227	1,568	H	24	•		
598-026D-0229	2,051	H	20	•		
598-026D-0230	2,076	H	16	•		
598-028D-0001	864	AAA	52		•	
598-028D-0025	1,587	B	248	•		
598-028D-0032	864	AAA	132			
598-032D-0002	920	AA	164	•	•	•
598-032D-0003	1,245	AA	160	•	•	•
598-032D-0005	994	AA	73	•	•	•
598-032D-0007	1,053	AA	199	•	•	•
598-032D-0009	1,199	AA	122	•	•	•
598-032D-0010	1,066	AA	151	•	•	•
598-032D-0011	1,103	AA	97	•	•	•
598-032D-0013	1,124	AA	92	•		
598-032D-0015	1,556	B	143	•		
598-032D-0033	1,484	A	228	•	•	•
598-034D-0013	1,493	A	244	•		
598-036D-0056	1,604	B	76	•		
598-037D-0001	1,703	B	133			
598-037D-0016	2,066	C	110	•		
598-037D-0017	829	AAA	49	•		
598-037D-0018	717	AAA	102	•		
598-037D-0019	581	AAA	98	•		
598-038D-0022	1,908	C	29	•		
598-038D-0025	1,710	B	10	•		
598-038D-0036	1,470	A	25	•		
598-038D-0053	1,328	A	21	•	•	
598-038D-0054	1,560	B	80	•		
598-040D-0028	828	AAA	58	•		
598-040D-0029	1,028	AA	89	•		
598-041D-0006	1,189	AA	17	•		
598-045D-0010	1,558	B	105	•		
598-045D-0012	976	AA	56	•		
598-045D-0013	1,085	AA	154	•		
598-045D-0014	987	AA	167	•		
598-045D-0016	1,107	AA	177	•		
598-045D-0017	954	AA	69	•		
598-045D-0018	858	AAA	187	•		
598-046D-0013	1,260	A	124			
598-046D-0024	2,207	D	182			
598-046D-0025	1,548	B	140			
598-046D-0031	1,693	B	172			
598-047D-0006	1,565	B	188			
598-047D-0014	1,670	B	206			
598-047D-0022	1,768	B	196			
598-047D-0105	1,543	G	230			
598-051D-0097	1,448	B	203	•		
598-052D-0012	1,365	A	139	•		
598-052D-0019	1,532	B	23	•		
598-052D-0020	1,553	B	12	•		
598-052D-0021	1,577	B	26	•		
598-052D-0051	1,929	C	18	•		
598-052D-0121	3,223	F	33		•	
598-053D-0030	1,657	B	116	•		
598-053D-0056	1,880	C	162	•		
598-053D-0058	1,818	C	47	•		
598-055D-0013	930	AA	181	•	•	
598-055D-0045	2,707	E	157	•	•	
598-055D-0046	1,934	C	32	•	•	
598-055D-0051	1,848	C	14	•	•	
598-055D-0063	1,397	A	149	•	•	
598-055D-0064	1,544	B	234	•	•	
598-055D-0099	1,872	C	236	•	•	
598-055D-0115	1,120	AA	240	•	•	
598-055D-0125	2,618	E	211	•	•	
598-057D-0011	1,366	A	70	•		
598-057D-0012	1,112	AA	118	•		
598-057D-0022	1,278	A	137	•		
598-057D-0023	1,674	B	131	•		
598-058D-0006	1,339	A	144	•	•	
598-058D-0007	1,013	AA	54	•	•	
598-058D-0010	676	AAA	45	•	•	
598-058D-0012	1,143	AA	40	•	•	
598-058D-0029	1,000	AA	250	•	•	
598-058D-0038	990	AA	108	•	•	
598-058D-0139	1,240	AAA	100	•	•	
598-061D-0001	1,747	B	113	•		
598-062D-0036	1,018	AA	109	•		•
598-062D-0058	1,108	AA	77	•	•	•
598-062D-0059	1,588	B	81	•	•	•
598-076D-0017	1,123	B	186	•		
598-076D-0018	1,116	B	146	•		
598-076D-0120	1,133	A	208	•		
598-077D-0038	1,650	C	214	•	•	
598-077D-0105	1,100	B	238	•		
598-077D-0106	1,200	B	87	•		
598-077D-0124	1,900	C	75	•	•	
598-077D-0139	1,800	C	242	•		
598-078D-0017	2,030	D	84	•		
598-078D-0036	1,035	D	88	•		
598-078D-0038	835	D	156	•		
598-080D-0002	796	AAA	179			•
598-080D-0008	1,644	B	13	•		
598-081D-0010	1,400	C	202	•	•	
598-081D-0021	1,536	C	220	•	•	
598-081D-0064	1,500	C	216	•		
598-087D-0003	1,067	D	191	•		
598-087D-0019	1,210	D	197	•		
598-087D-0022	1,224	D	224	•		
598-087D-0071	1,437	E	155	•		
598-087D-0087	1,539	F	120	•		
598-089D-0052	1,409	C	72	•		
598-099D-0012	2,270	D	114	•		
598-099D-0020	2,360	D	129	•	•	
598-099D-0024	1,898	C	106	•		
598-099D-0026	1,388	C	119	•		
598-106D-0003	1,250	B	111		•	•
598-106D-0007	1,382	B	79		•	•
598-106D-0023	2,647	D	90			•

Once you find the home plan you've been looking for, here are some suggestions on how to make your Dream Home a reality. To get started, order the type of plans that fit your particular situation.

Your Choices:

The 1-Set Package - We offer a 1-set plan package so you can study your home in detail. This one set is considered a study set and is marked "not for construction." It is a copyright violation to reproduce blueprints.

The Minimum 5-Set Package - If you're ready to start the construction process, this 5-set package is the minimum number of blueprint sets you will need. It will require keeping close track of each set so they can be used by multiple subcontractors and tradespeople.

The Standard 8-Set Package - For best results in terms of cost, schedule and quality of construction, we recommend you order eight (or more) sets of blueprints. Besides one set for yourself, additional sets of blueprints will be required by your mortgage lender, local building department, general contractor and all subcontractors working on foundation, electrical, plumbing, heating/air conditioning, carpentry work, etc.

Reproducible Masters - If you wish to make some minor design changes, you'll want to order reproducible masters. These drawings contain the same information as the blueprints but are printed on reproducible paper that is easy to alter and clearly indicates your right to copy or reproduce. This will allow your builder or a local design professional to make the necessary drawing changes without the major expense of redrawing the plans. This package also allows you to print copies of the modified plans as needed. The right of building only one structure from these plans is licensed exclusively to the buyer. You may not use this design to build a second or multiple dwellings without purchasing another blueprint. Each violation of the Copyright Law is punishable in a fine.

Mirror Reverse Sets - Plans can be printed in mirror reverse. These plans are useful when the house would fit your site better if all the rooms were on the opposite side than shown. They are simply a mirror image of the original drawings causing the lettering and dimensions to read backwards. Therefore, when ordering mirror reverse drawings, you must purchase at least one set of right-reading plans. Some of our plans are offered mirror reverse right-reading. This means the plan, lettering and dimensions are flipped but read correctly. See the Home Plan Index on page 252 for availability.

Other Great Products...

The Legal Kit - Avoid many legal pitfalls and build your home with confidence using the forms and contracts featured in this kit. Included are request for proposal documents, various fixed price and cost plus contracts, instructions on how and when to use each form, warranty statements and more. Save time and money before you break ground on your new home or start a remodeling project. All forms are reproducible. The kit is ideal for homebuilders and contractors. Cost: $35.00

Detail Plan Packages - Electrical, Plumbing and Framing Packages - Three separate packages offer homebuilders details for constructing various foundations; numerous floor, wall and roof framing techniques; simple to complex residential wiring; sump and water softener hookups; plumbing connection methods; installation of septic systems, and more. Each package includes three dimensional illustrations and a glossary of terms. Purchase one or all three. Note: These drawings do not pertain to a specific home plan. Cost: $20.00 each or all three for $40.00

More Helpful Building Aids

Your Blueprint Package contains the necessary construction information to build your home. We also offer the following products and services to save you time and money in the building process.

Express Delivery - Most orders are processed within 24 hours of receipt. Please allow 7-10 business days for delivery. If you need to place a rush order, please call us by 11:00 a.m. Monday-Friday CST and ask for express service (allow 1-2 business days).

Technical Assistance - If you have questions, please call our technical support line at 1-314-770-2228 between 8:00 a.m. and 5:00 p.m. Monday-Friday CST. Whether it involves design modifications or field assistance, our designers are extremely familiar with all of our designs and will be happy to help you. We want your home to be everything you expect it to be.

Material List - Material lists are available for many of the plans in this publication. Each list gives you the quantity, dimensions and description of the building materials necessary to construct your home. You'll get faster and more accurate bids from your contractor while saving money by paying for only the materials you need. See the Home Plan Index on page 252 for availability. Note: Material lists are not refundable. Cost: $125.00

We understand that it is difficult to find blueprints for a home that will meet all your needs. That is why HDA, Inc. (Home Design Alternatives) is pleased to offer home plan modification services.

Typical home plan modifications include:

- Changing foundation type
- Adding square footage to a plan
- Changing the entry into a garage
- Changing a two-car garage to a three-car garage or making a garage larger
- Redesigning kitchen, baths, and bedrooms
- Changing exterior elevations
- Or most other home plan modifications you may desire!

Some home plan modifications we cannot make include:

- Reversing the plans
- Adapting/engineering plans to meet your local building codes
- Combining parts of two different plans (due to copyright laws)

Our plan modification service is easy to use. Simply:

1. Decide on the modifications you want. For the most accurate quote, be as detailed as possible and refer to rooms in the same manner as the floor plan (i.e. if the floor plan refers to a "den," use "den" in your description). Including a sketch of the modified floor plan is always helpful.

2. Complete and e-mail the modification request form that can be found online at www.houseplansandmore.com.

3. Within two business days, you will receive your quote. Quotes do not include the cost of the reproducible masters required for our designer to legally make changes.

4. Call to accept the quote and purchase the reproducible masters. For example, if your quote is $850 and the reproducible masters for your plan are $800, your order total will be $1650 plus two shipping and handling charges (one to ship the reproducible masters to our designer and one to ship the modified plans to you).

5. Our designer will send you up to three drafts to verify your initial changes. Extra costs apply after the third draft. If additional changes are made that alter the original request, extra charges may be incurred.

6. Once you approve a draft with the final changes, we then make the changes to the reproducible masters by adding additional sheets. The original reproducible masters (with no changes) plus your new changed sheets will be shipped to you.

Other Important Information:

- Plans cannot be redrawn in reverse format. All modifications will be made to match the reproducible master's original layout. Once you receive the plans, you can make reverse copies at your local blueprint shop.

- Our staff designer will provide the first draft for your review within 4 weeks (plus shipping time) of receiving your order.
  - You will receive up to three drafts to review before your original changes are modified. The first draft will totally encompass all modifications based on your original request. Additional changes not included in your original request will be charged separately at an hourly rate of $75 or a flat quoted rate.

- Modifications will be drawn on a separate sheet with the changes shown and a note to see the main sheet for details. For example, a floor plan sheet from the original set (i.e. Sheet 3) would be followed by a new floor plan sheet with changes (i.e. Sheet A-3).

- Plans are drawn to meet national building codes. Modifications will not be drawn to any particular state or county codes, thus we cannot guarantee that the revisions will meet your local building codes. You may be required to have a local architect or designer review the plans in order to have them comply with your state or county building codes.

- Time and cost estimates are good for 90 calendar days.

- All modification requests need to be submitted in writing. Verbal requests will not be accepted.

2 Easy Steps for FAST service

1. Visit www.houseplansandmore.com to download the modification request form.

2. E-mail the completed form to customize@hdainc.com or fax to 913-856-7751.

   If you are not able to access the internet, please call 1-800-373-2646 (Monday-Friday, 8am-5pm CST).